AF479379

frost

For Brigitta Maria

Hans Danuser **frost** Scalo Zürich-Berlin-New York

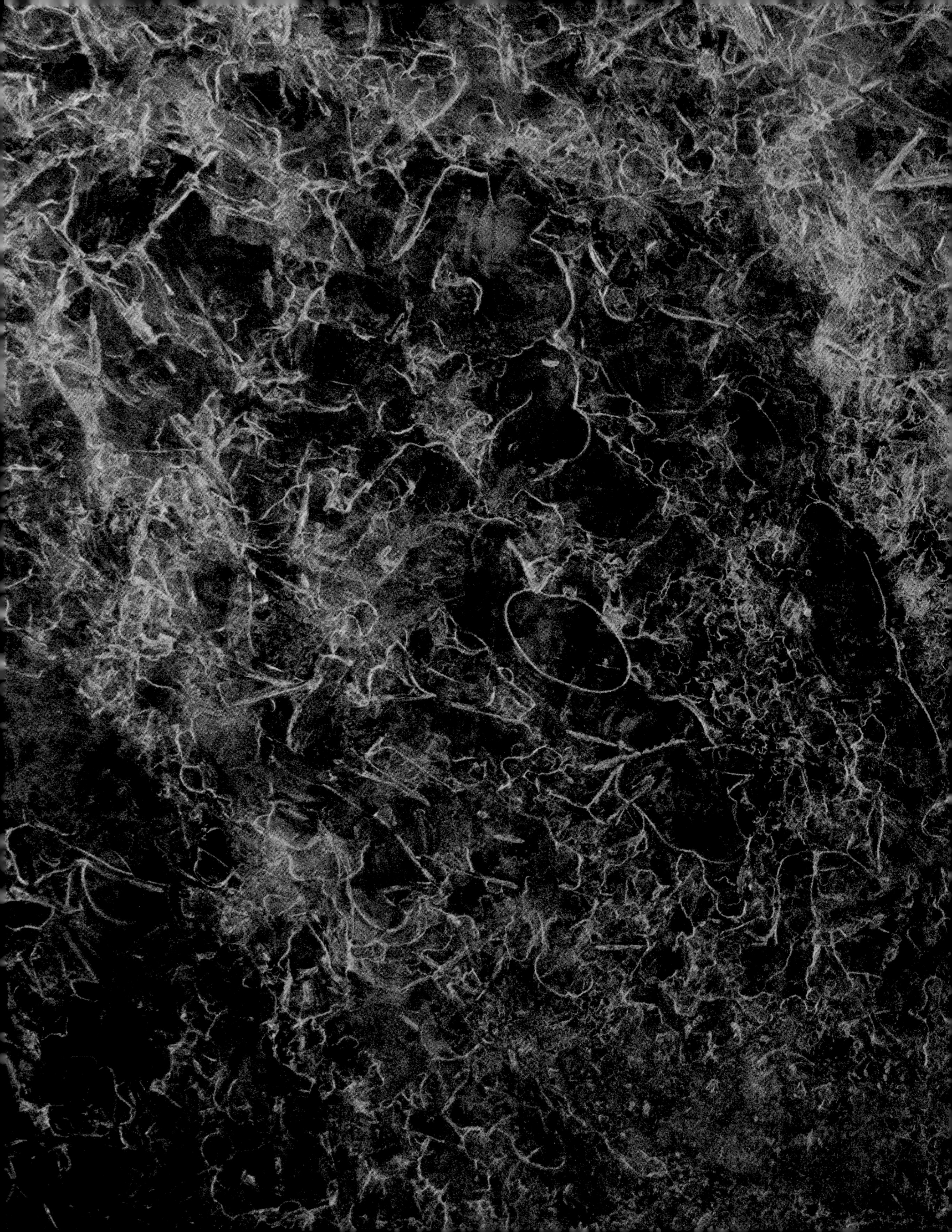

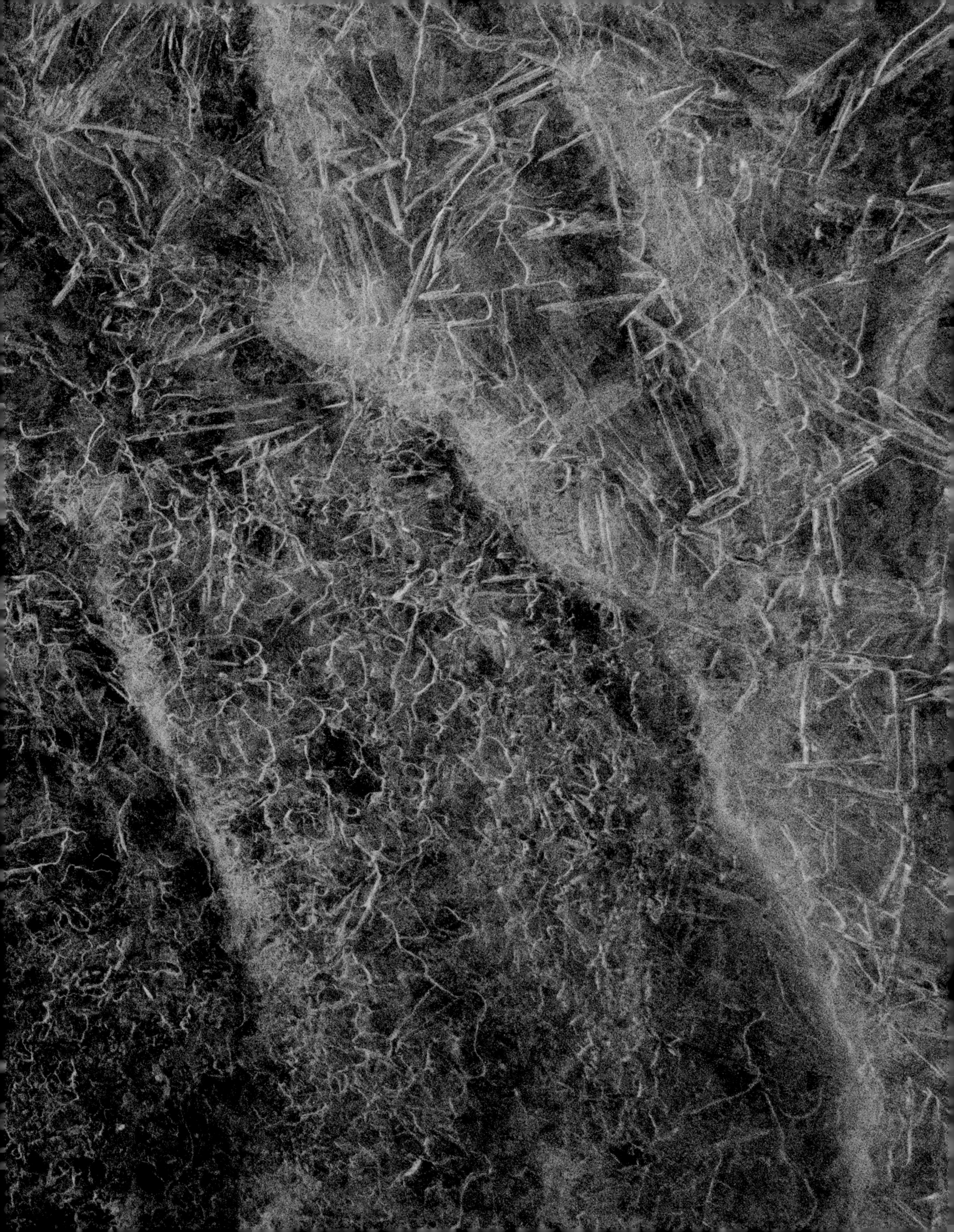

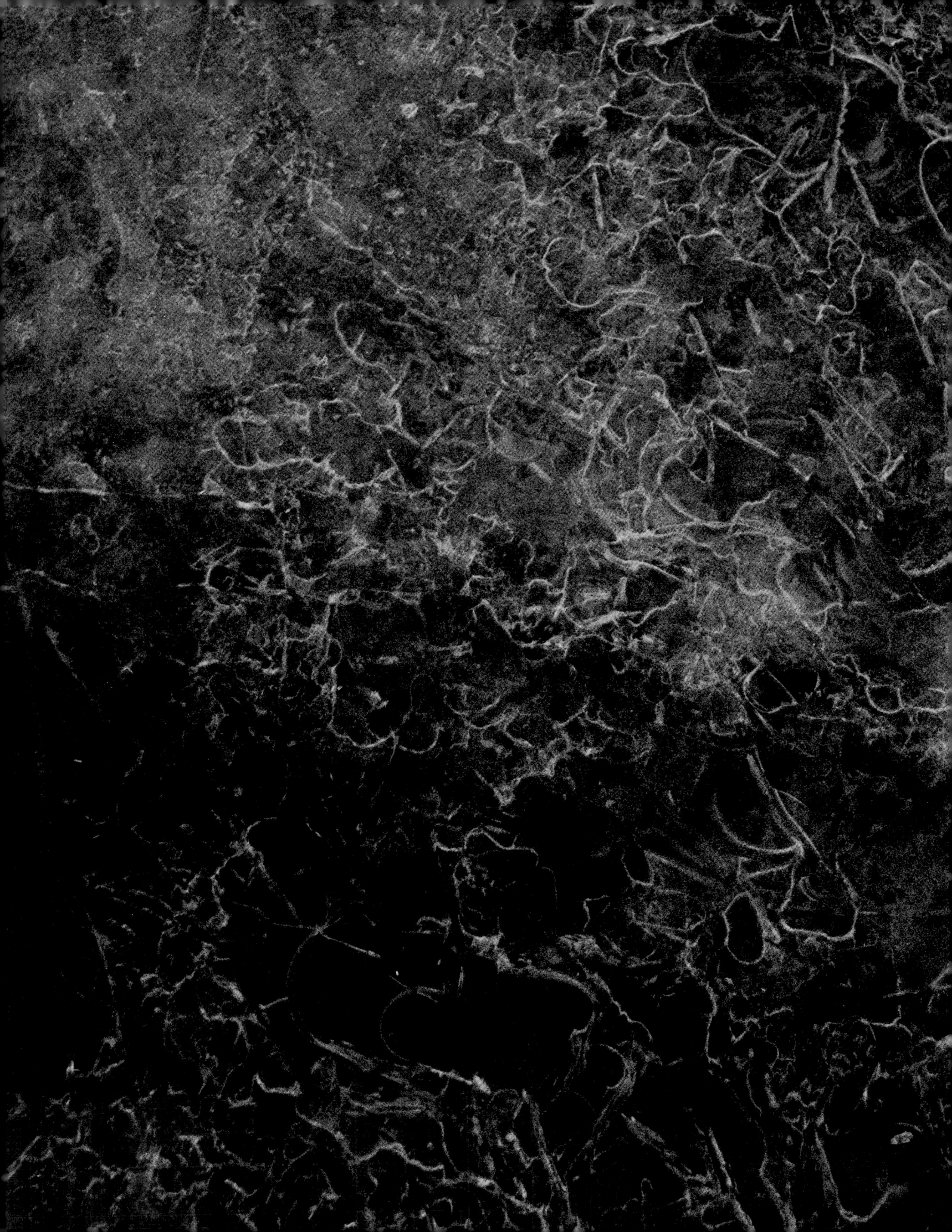

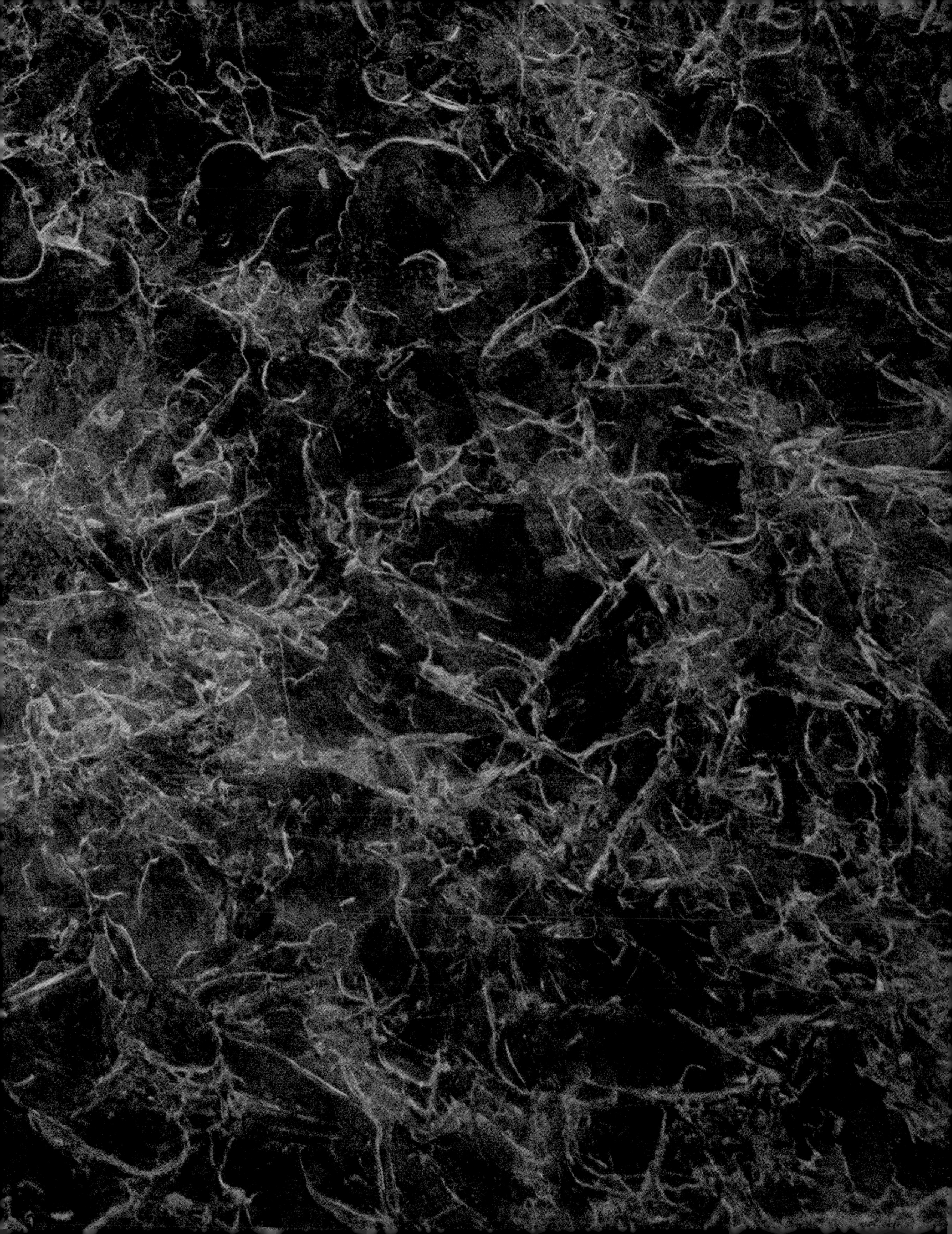

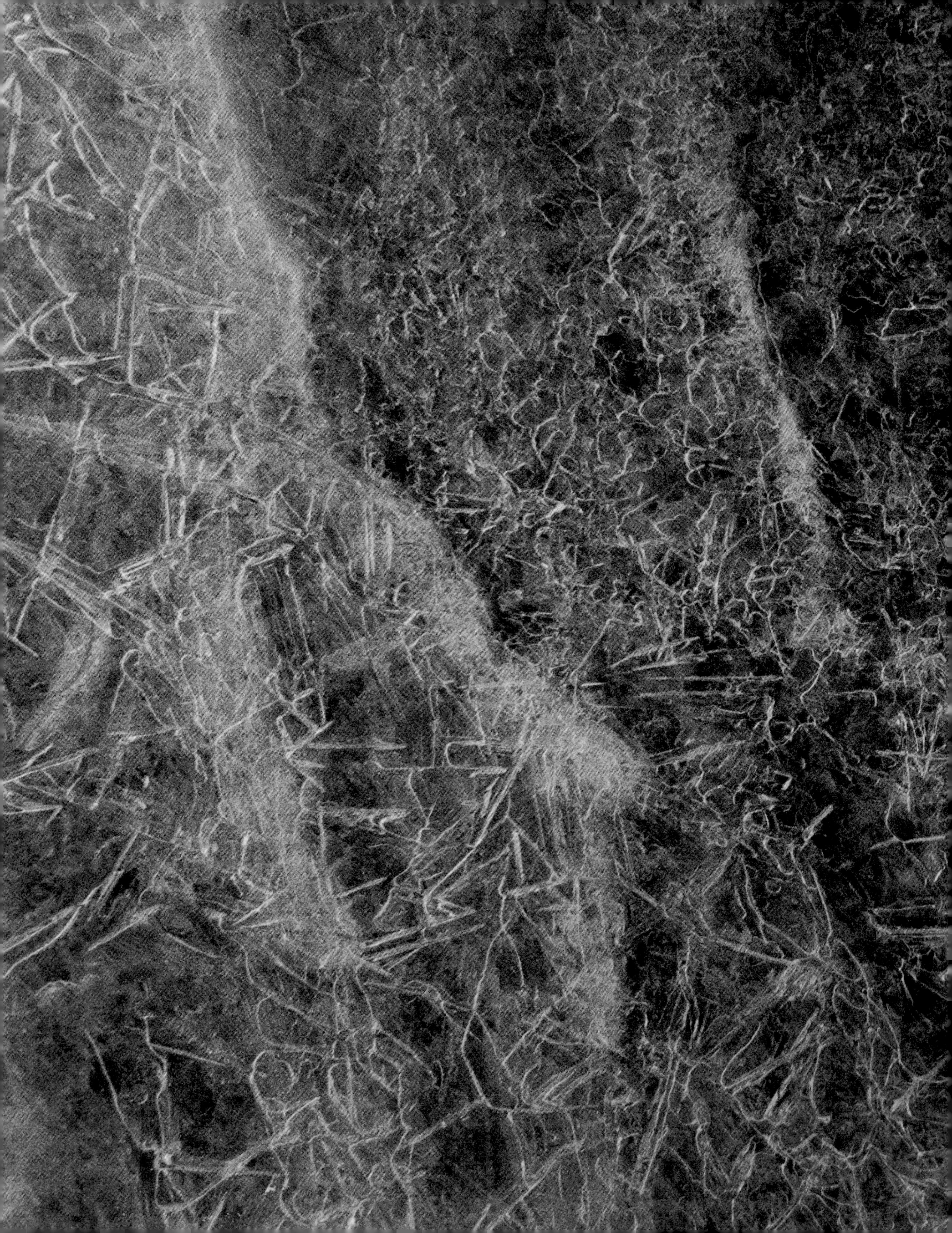

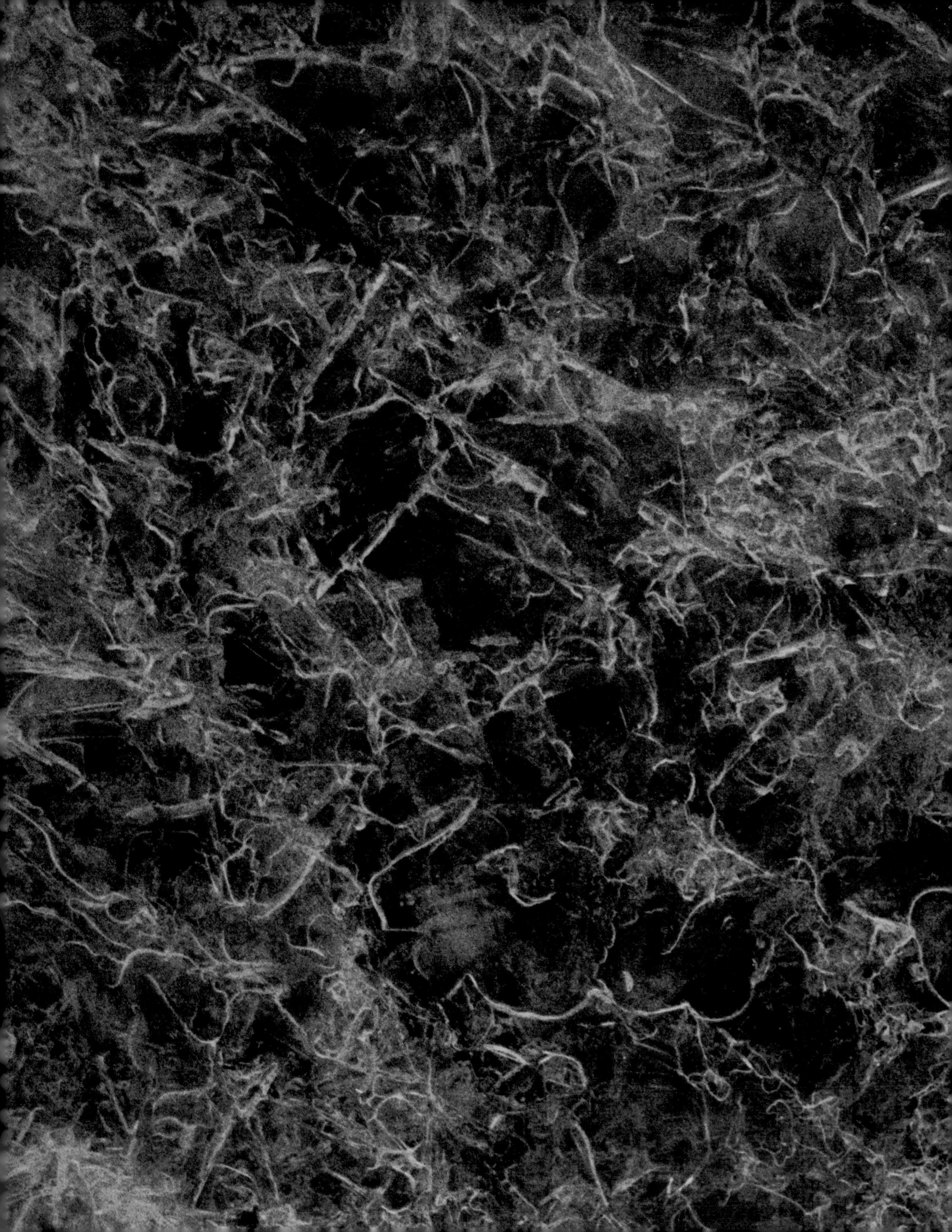

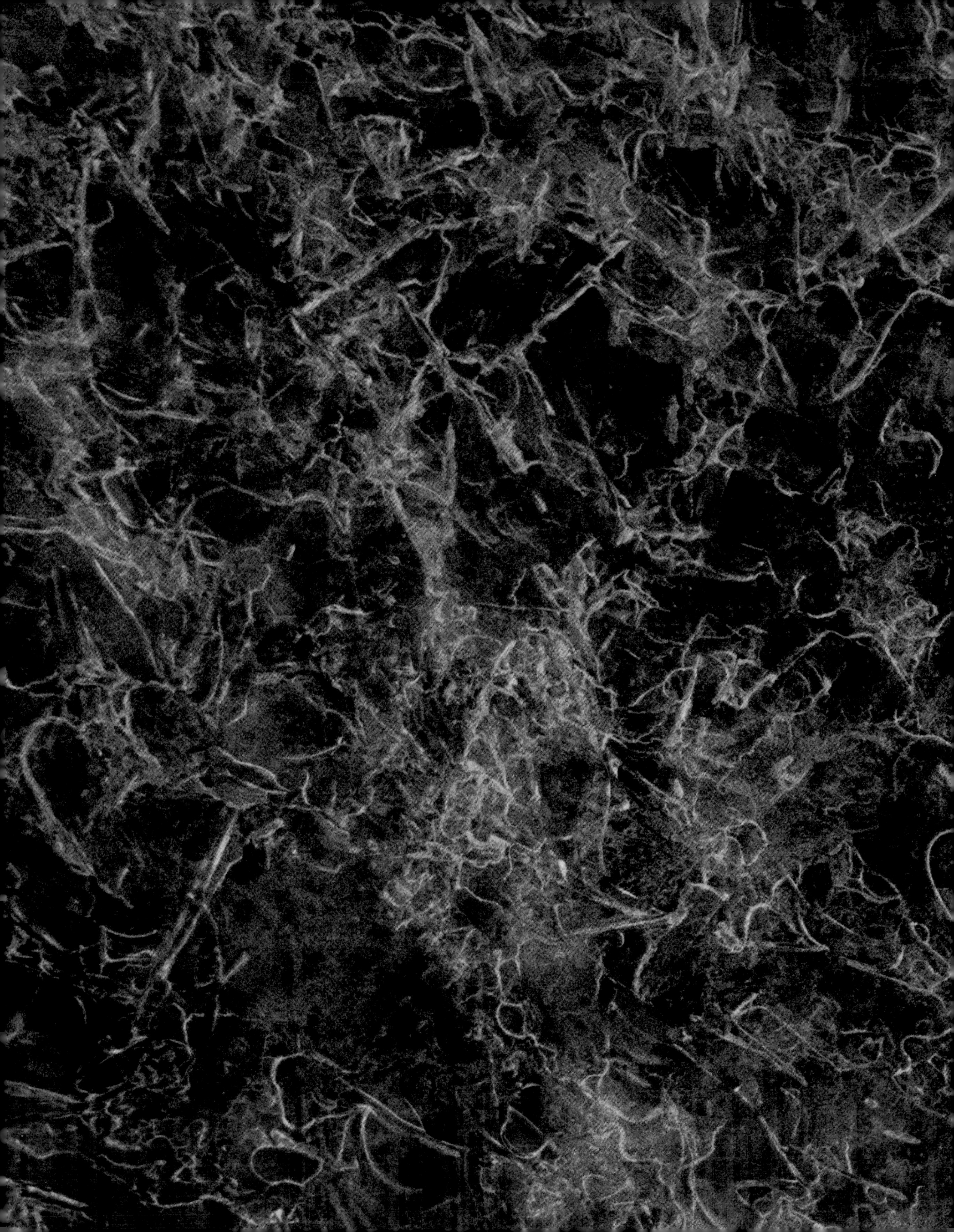

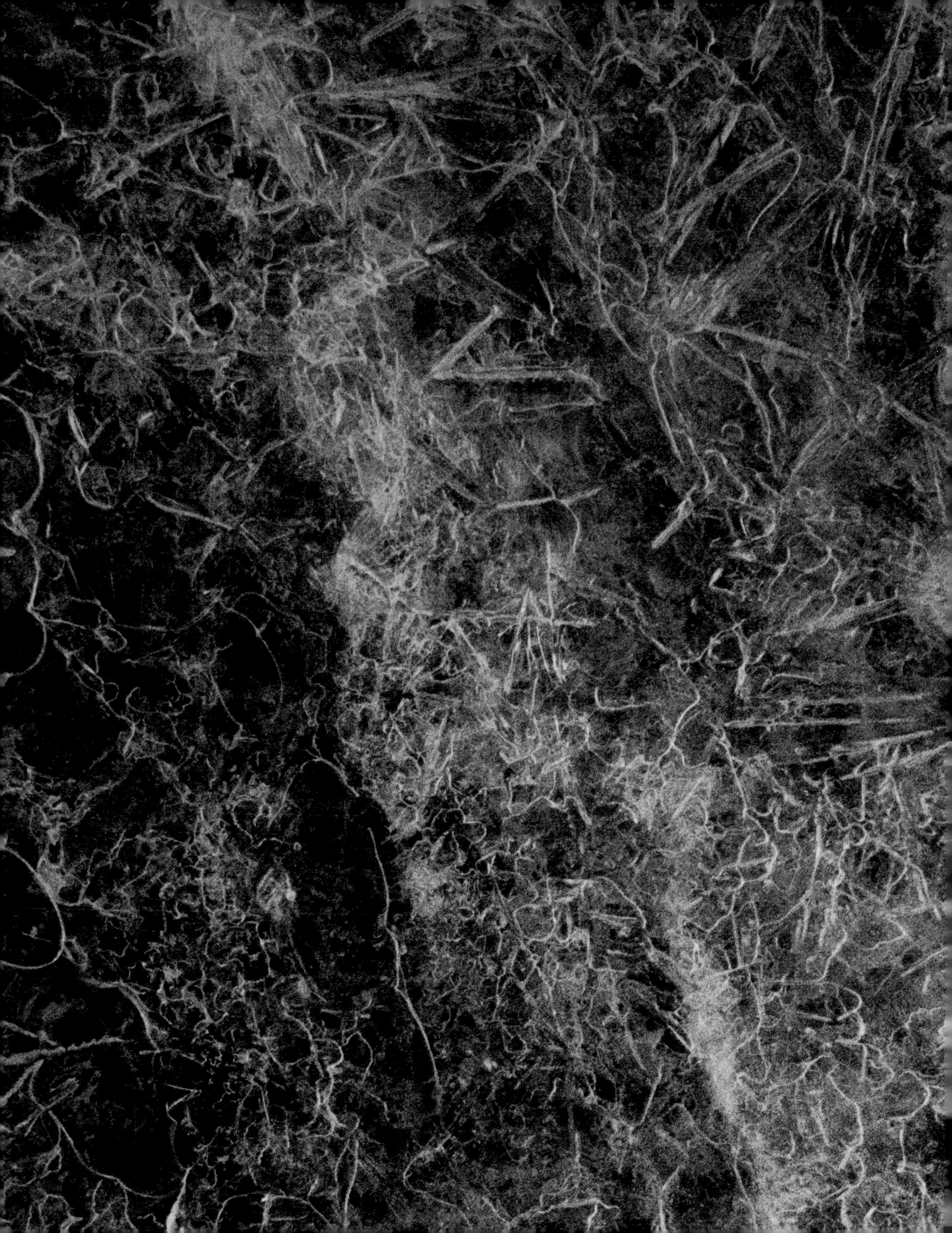

am,

stram,

gram,

pick d

am

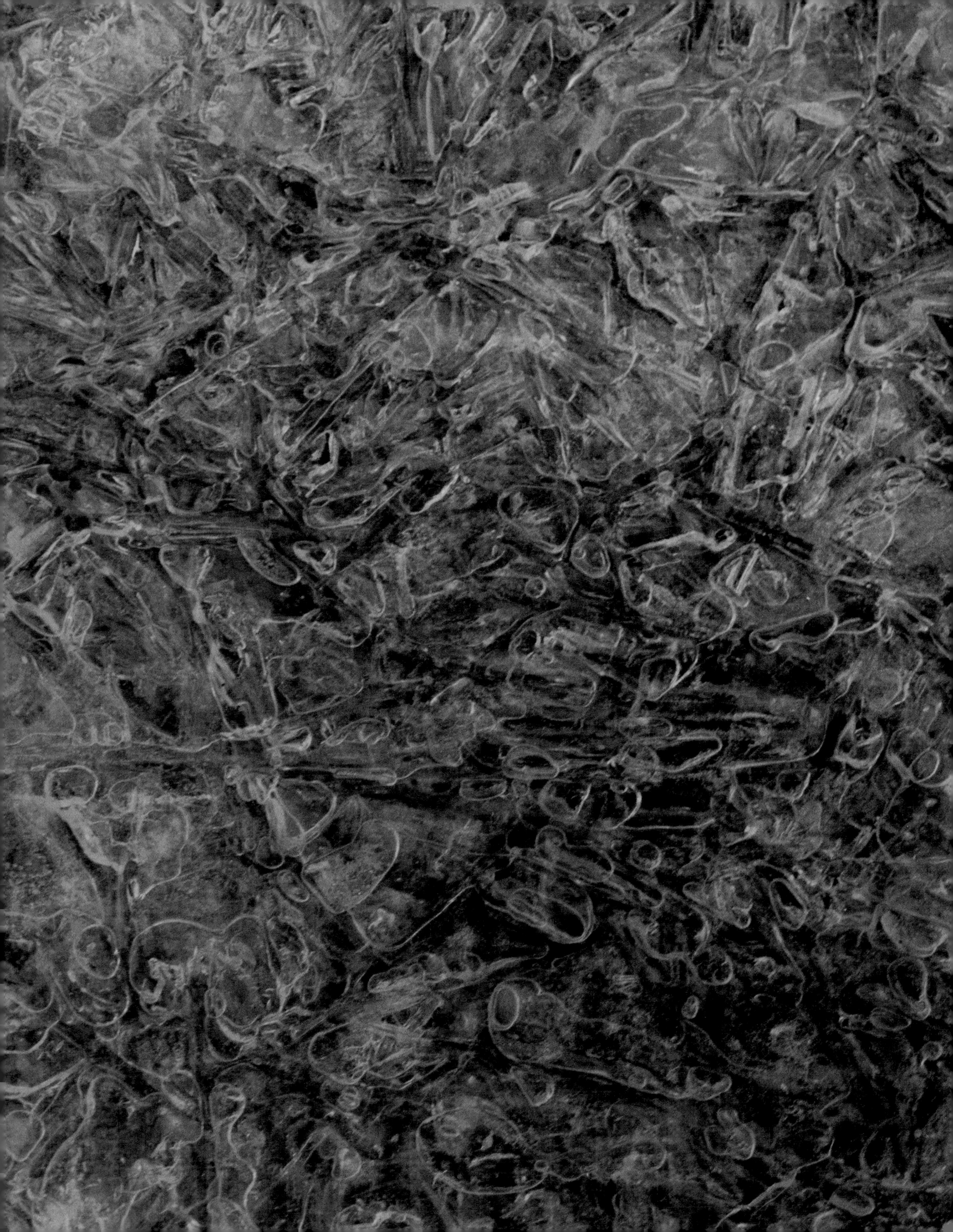

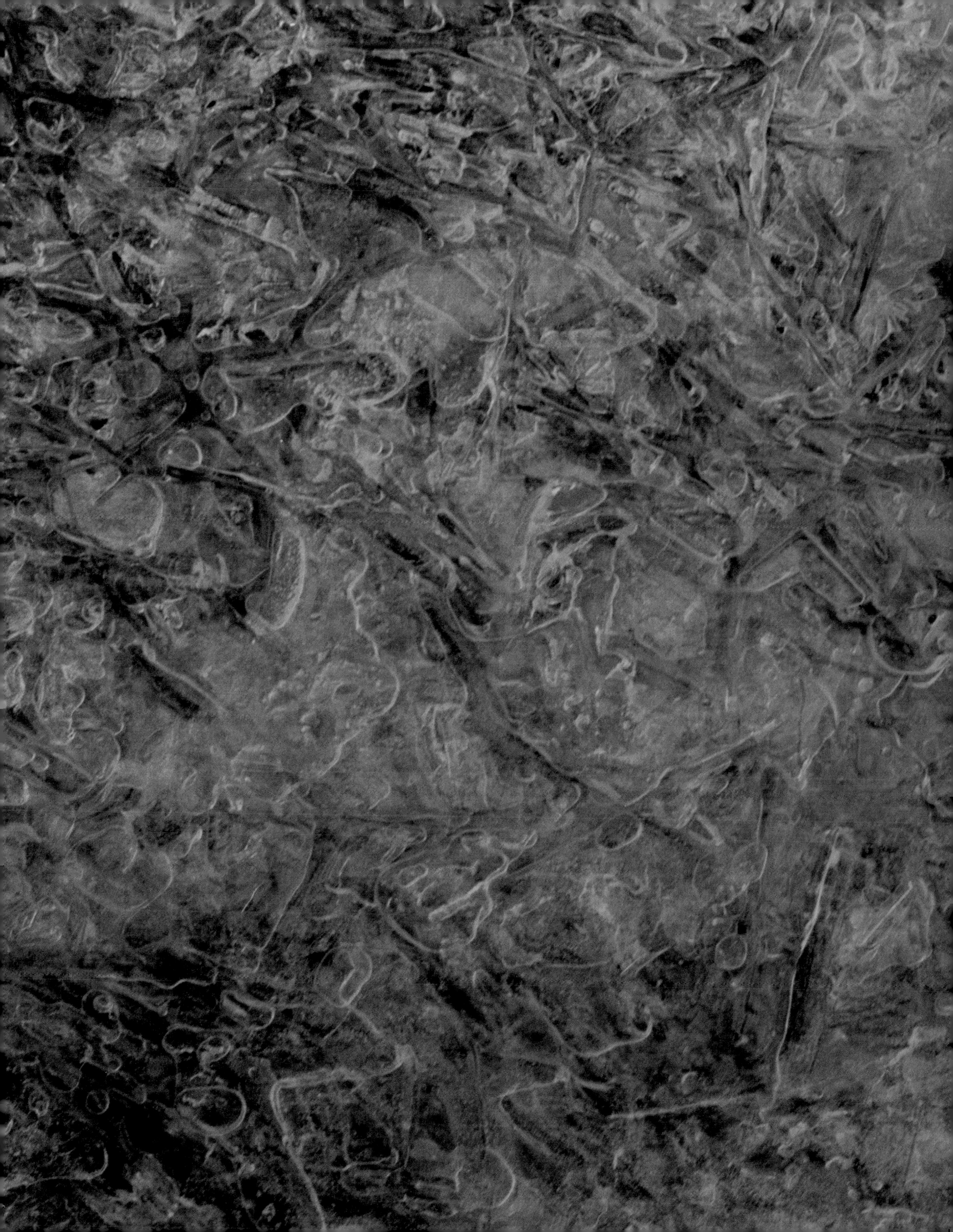

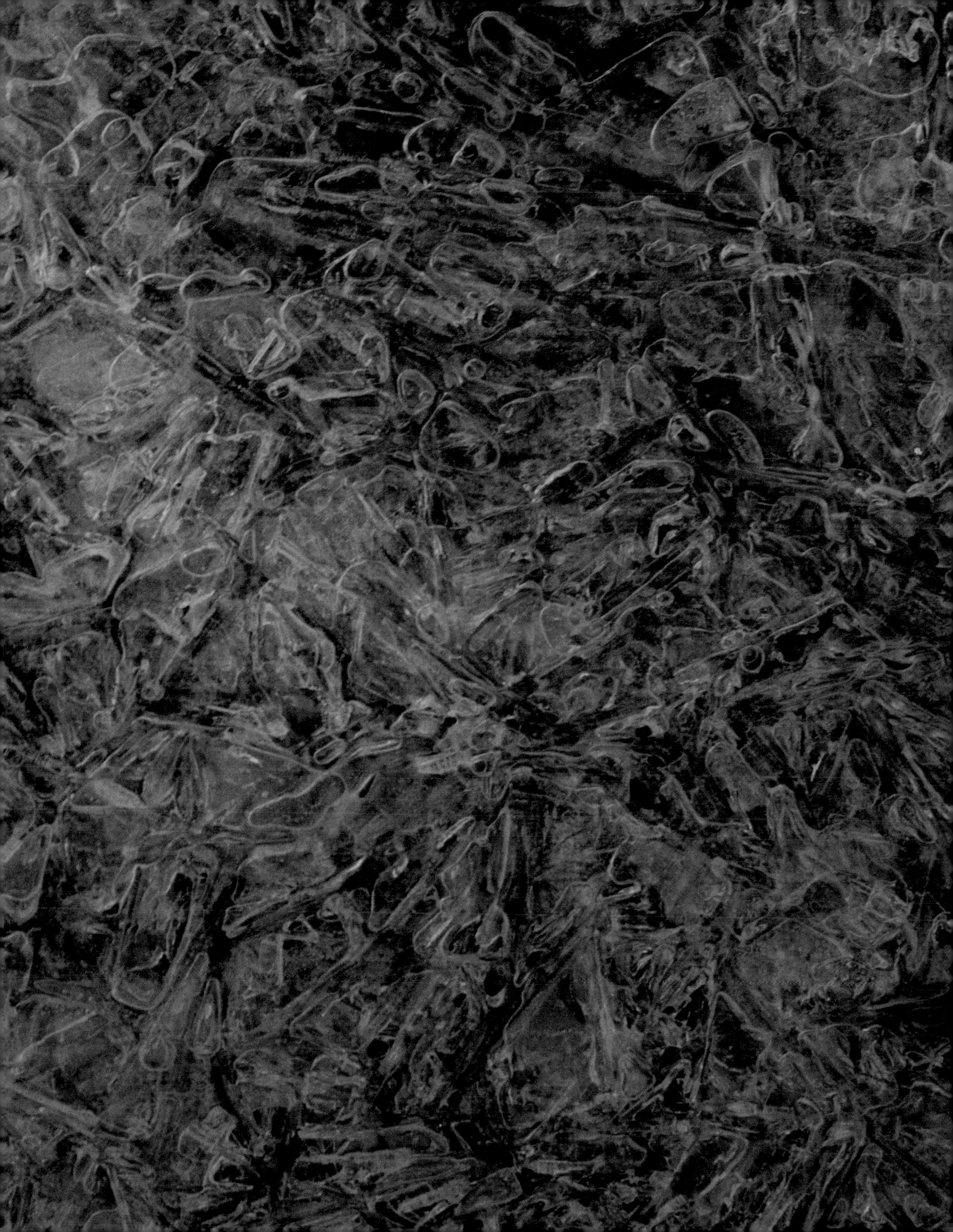

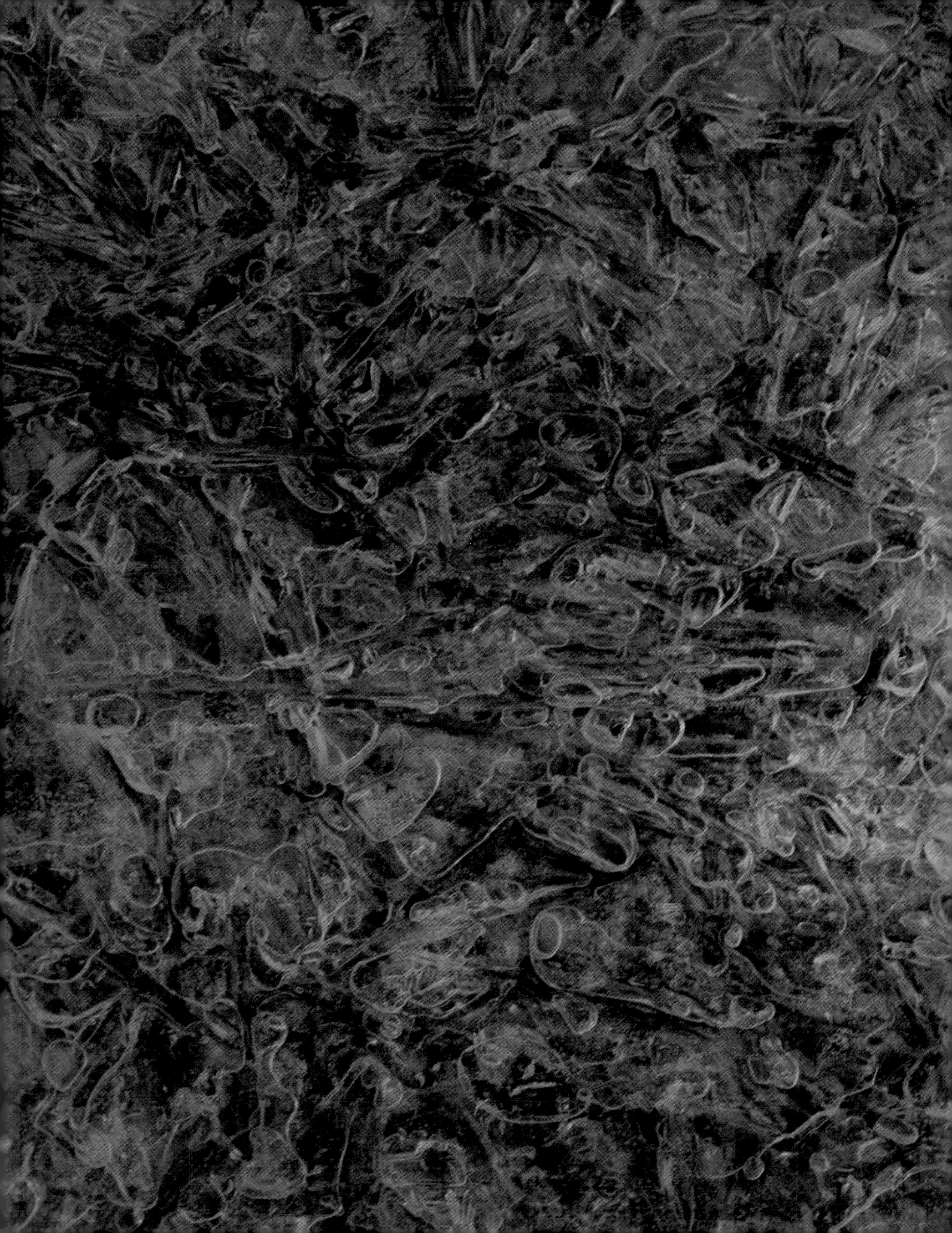

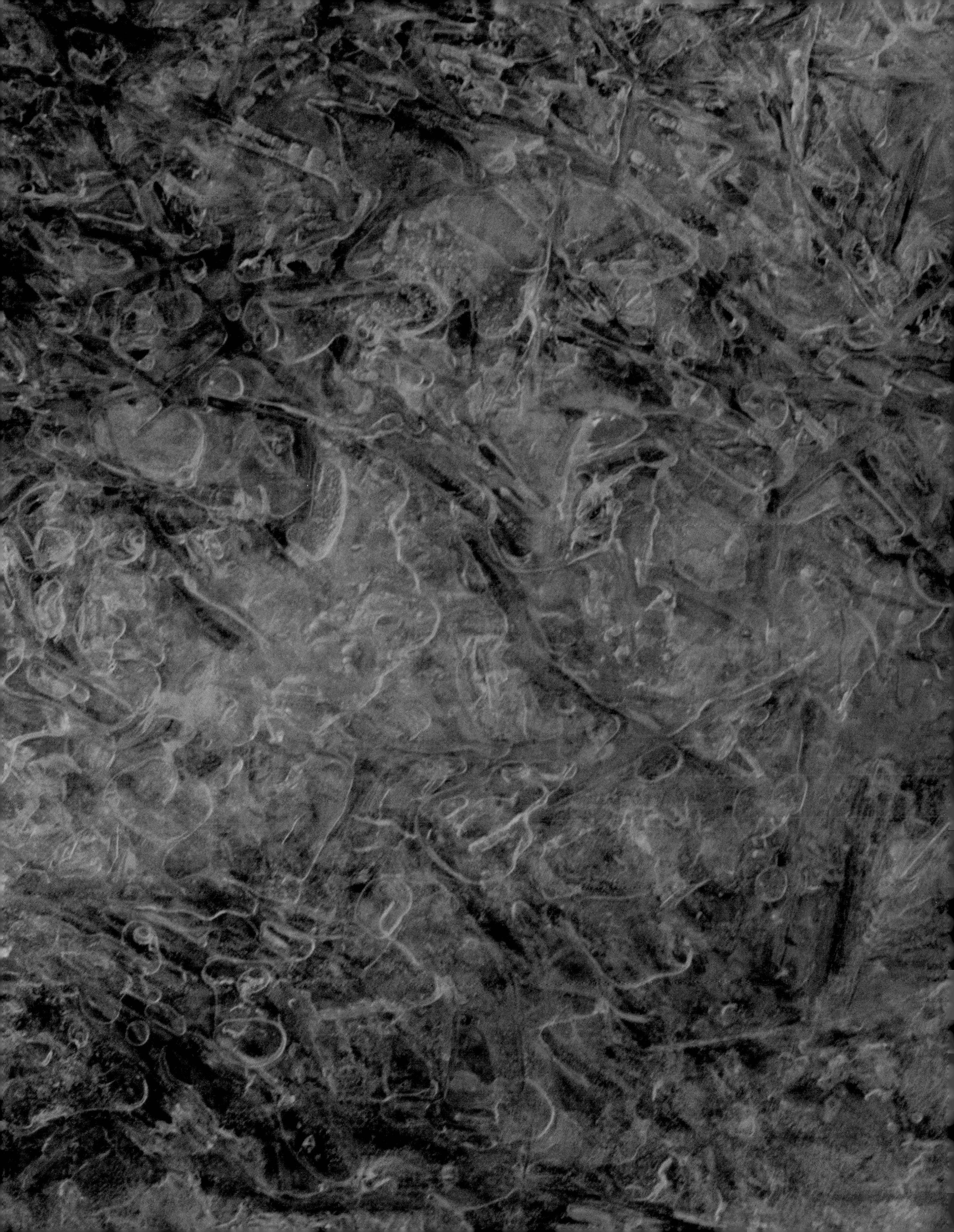

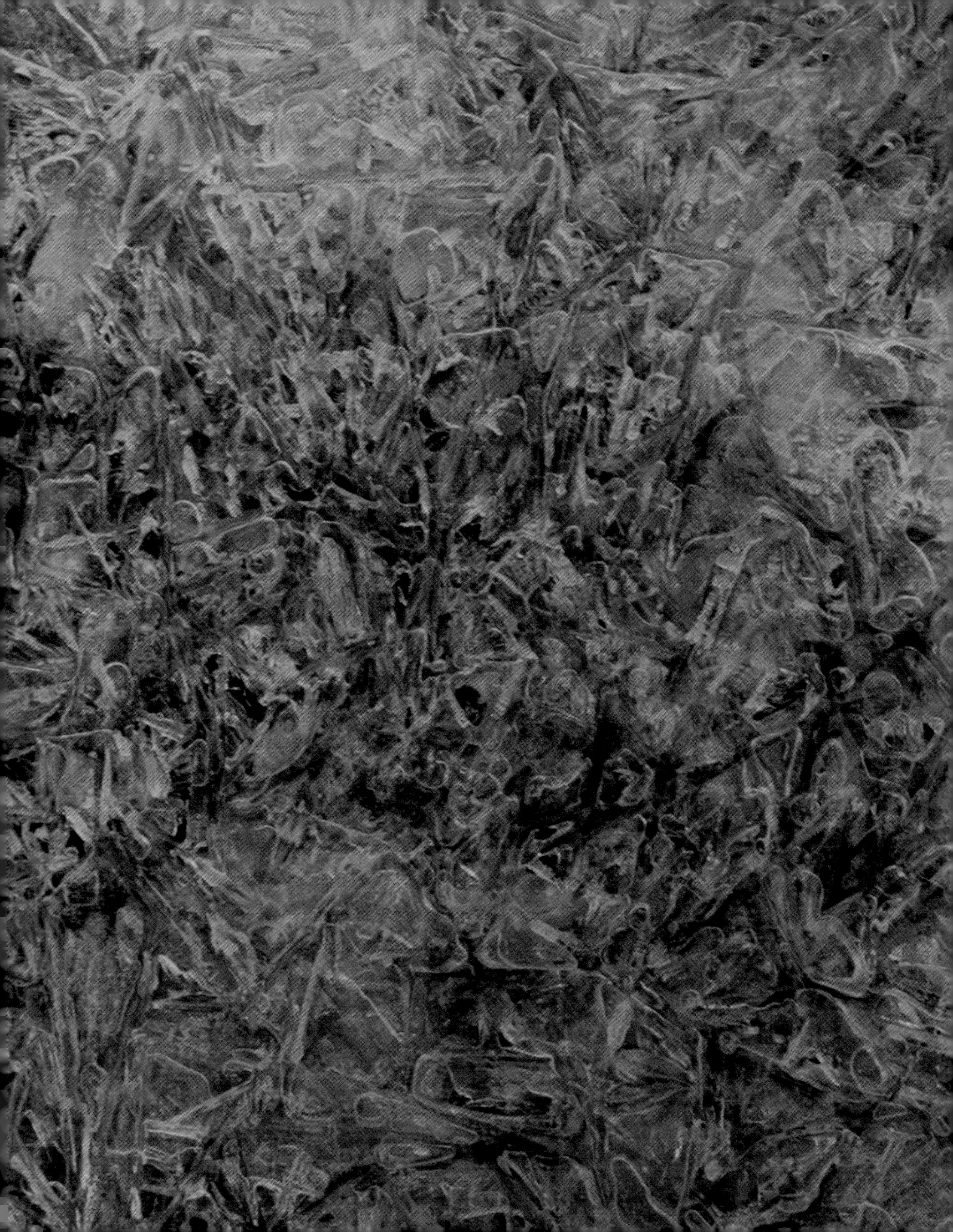

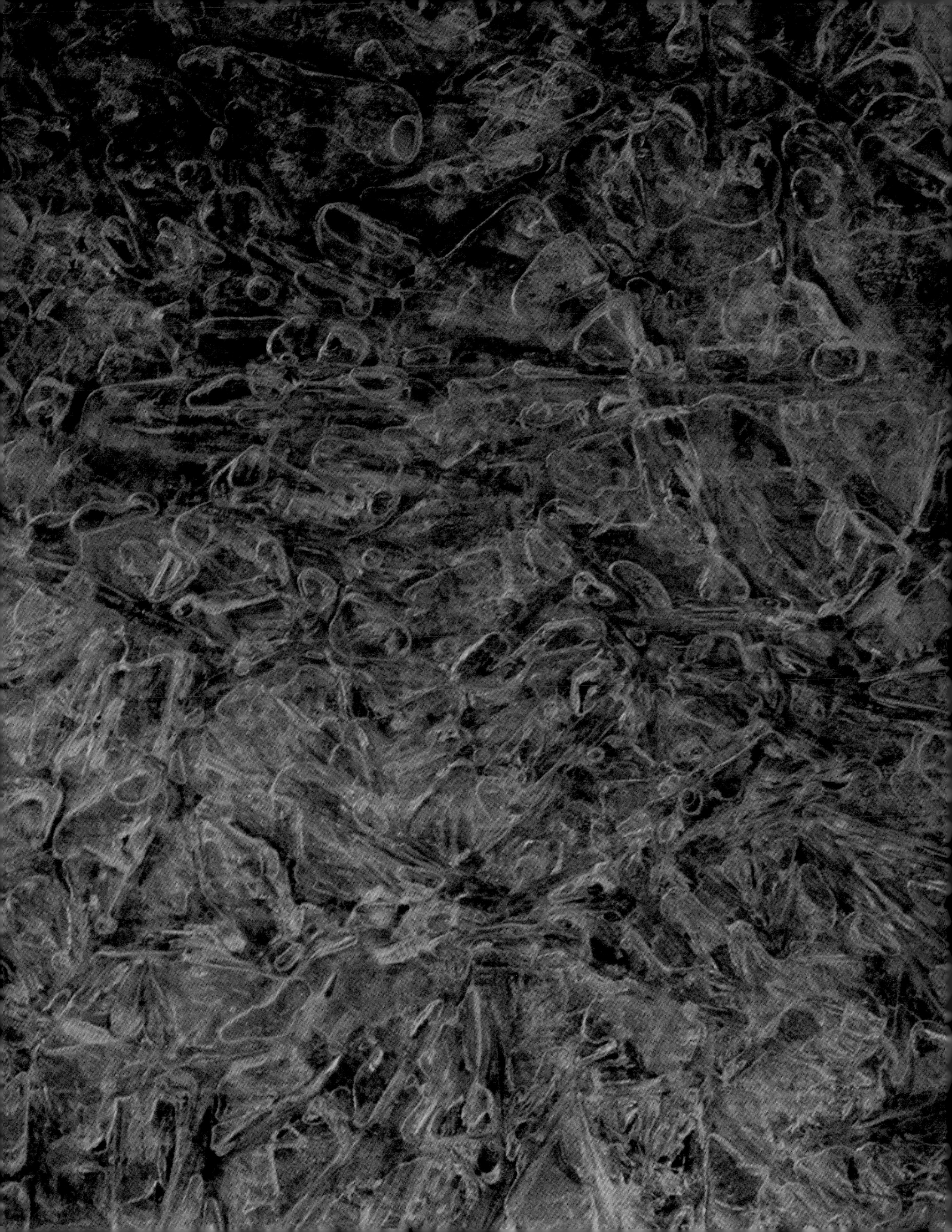

eenie,

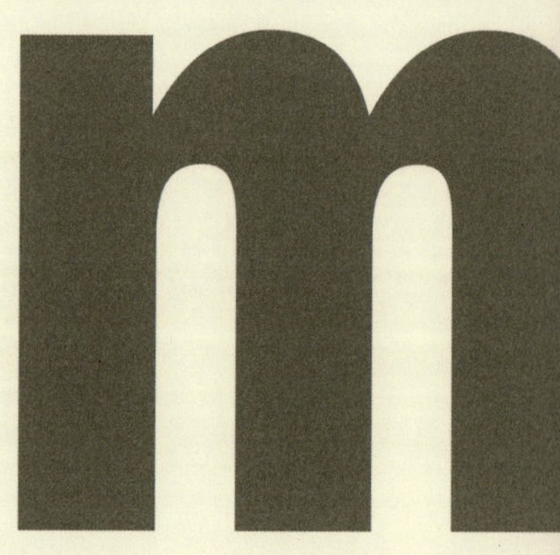

eenie,

min

ey, mo

snipp,

snapp,

snute,

du

er ute

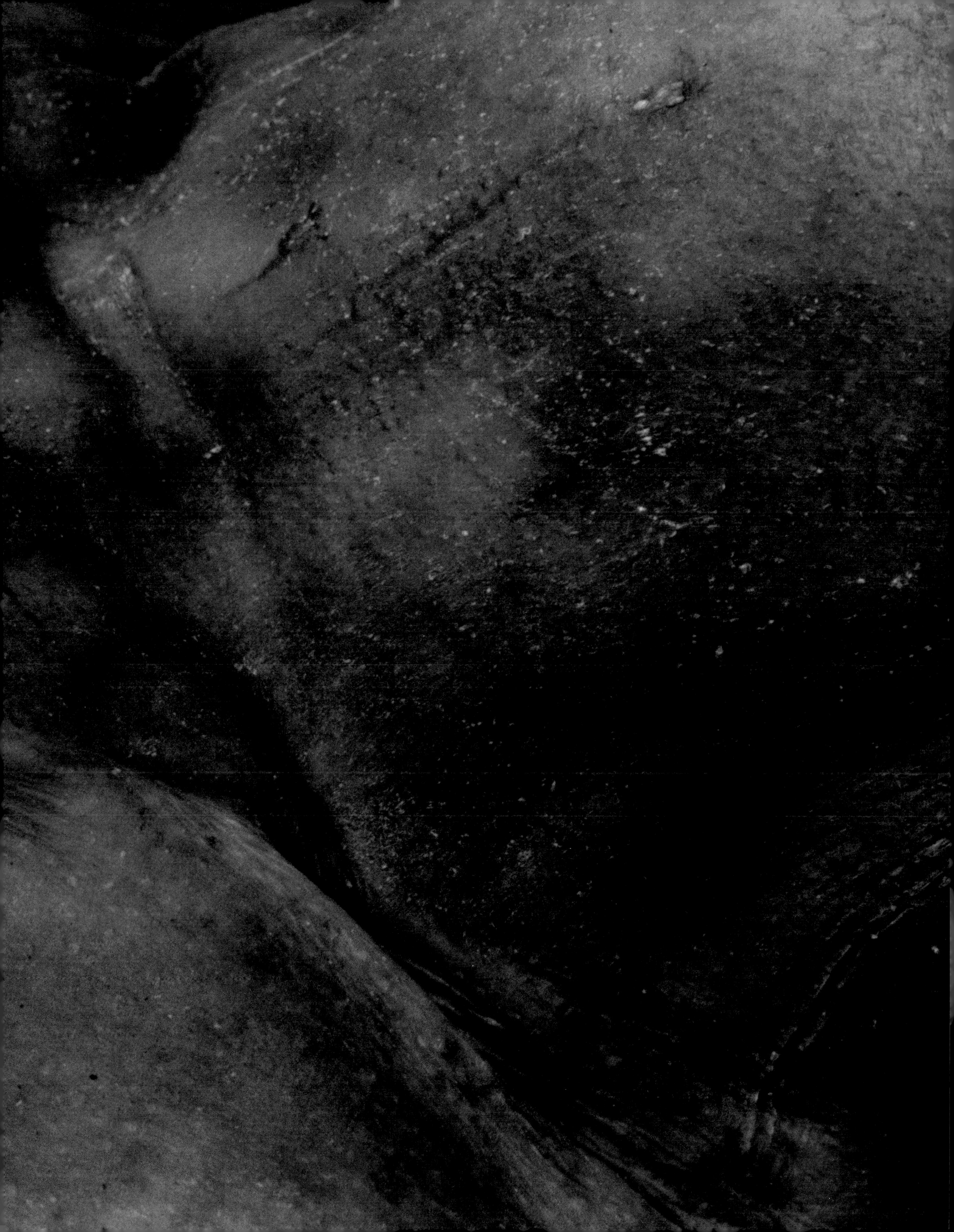

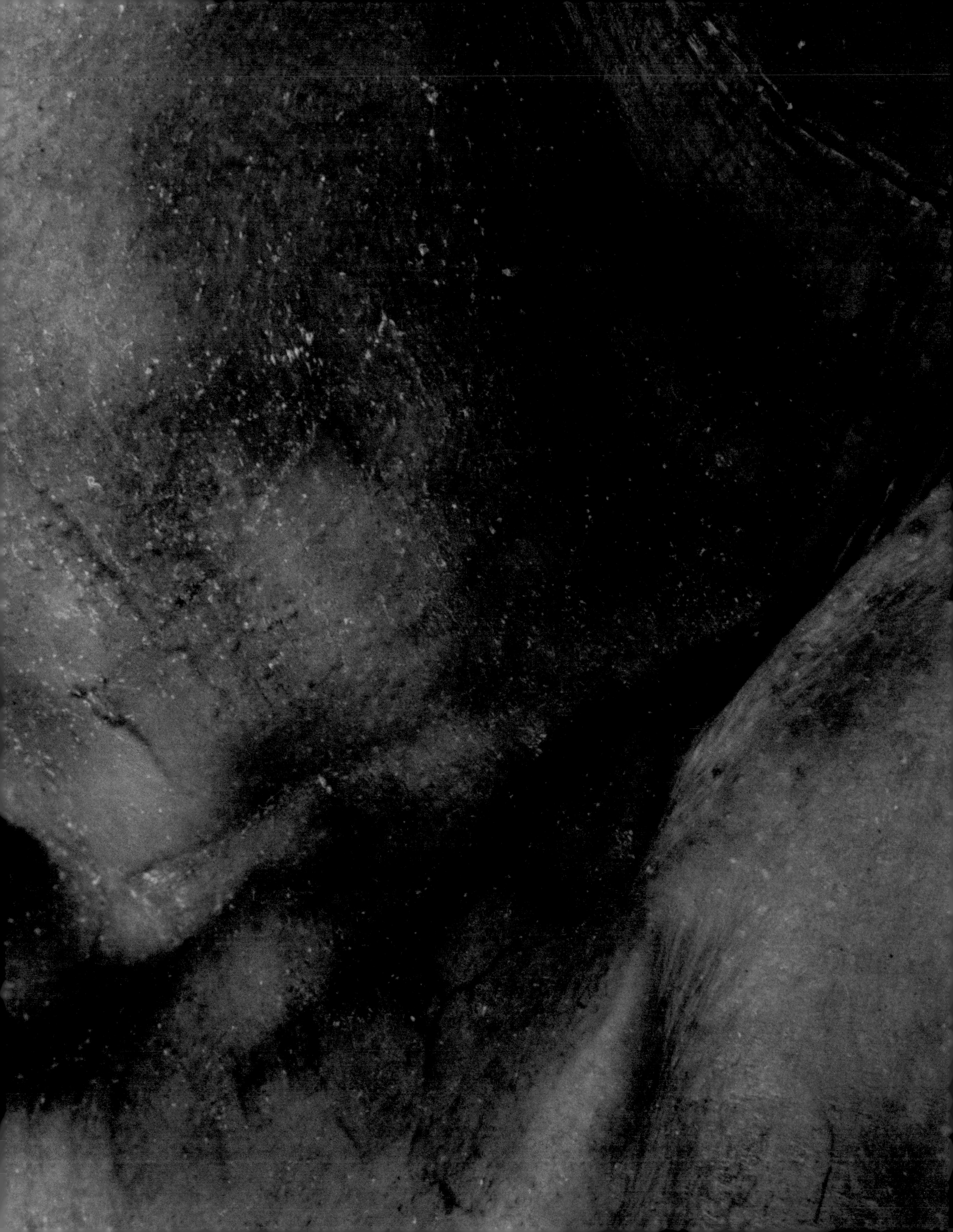

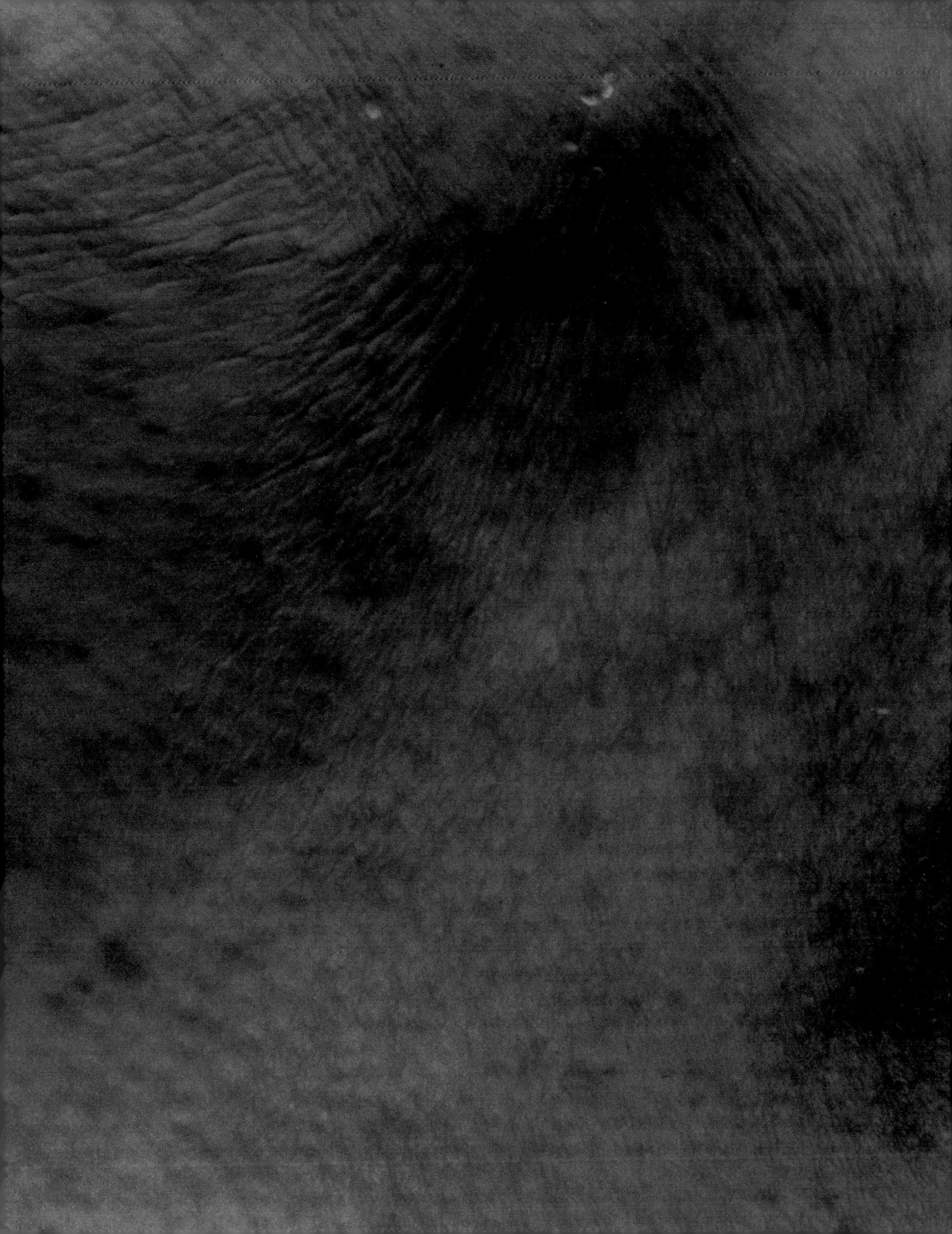

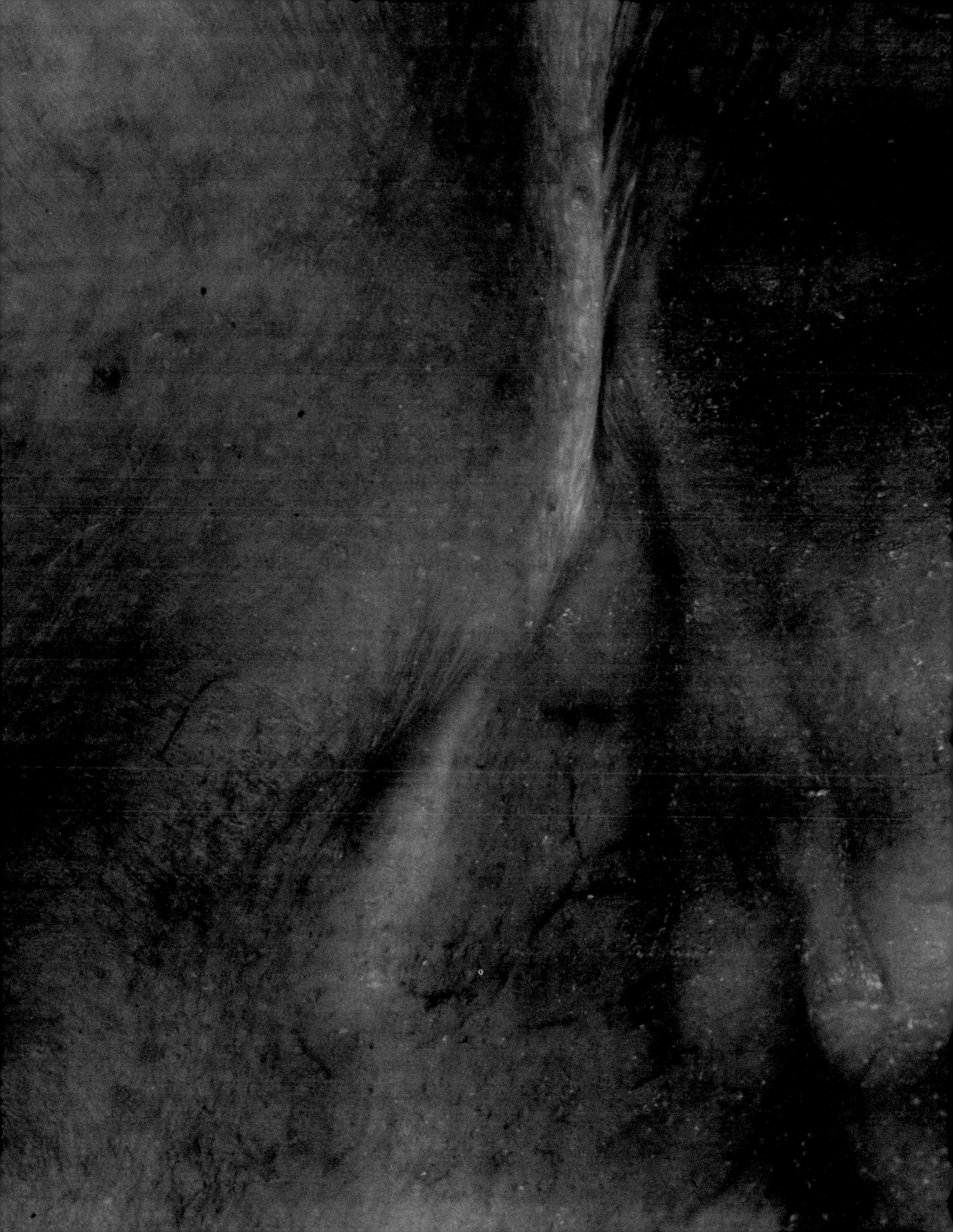

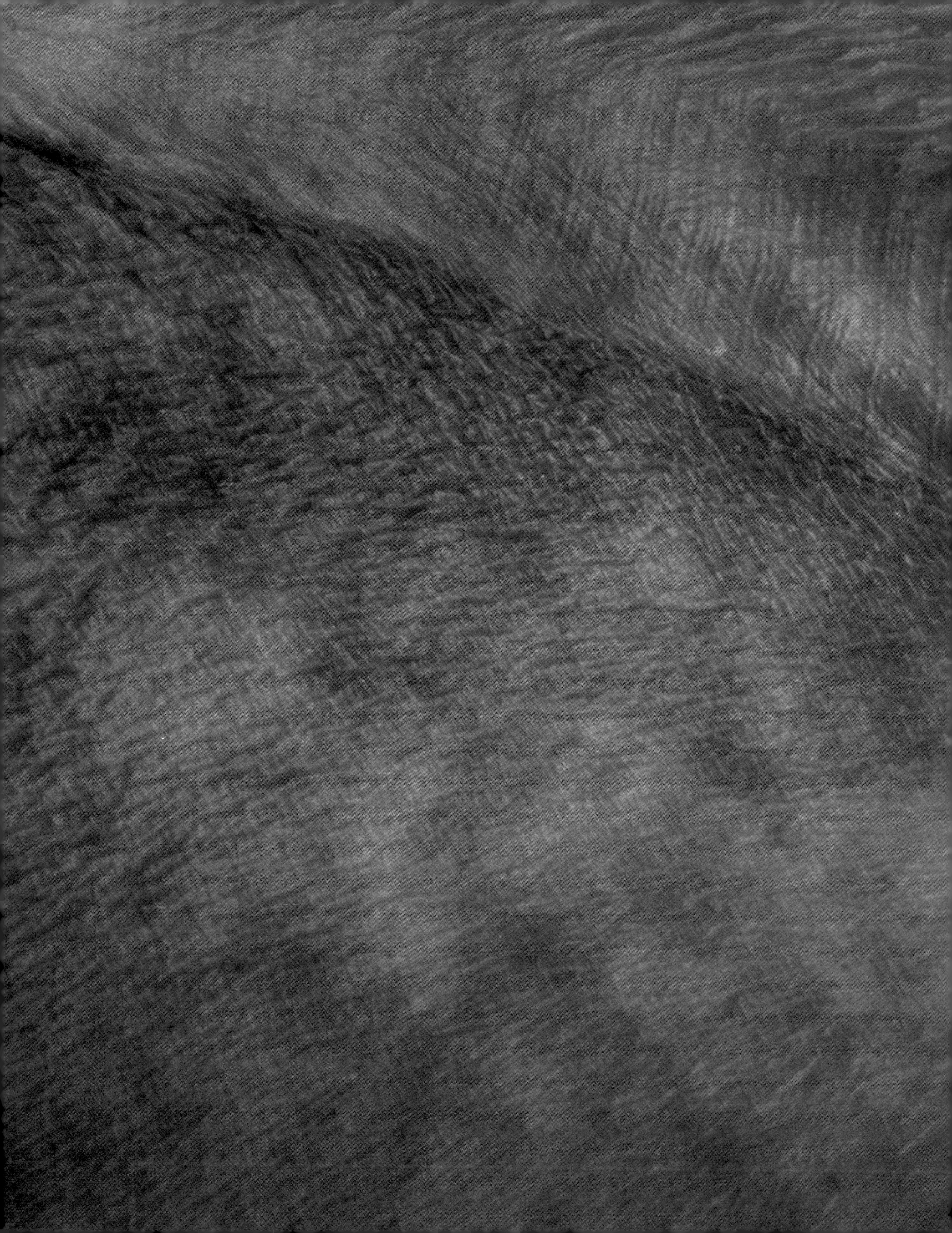

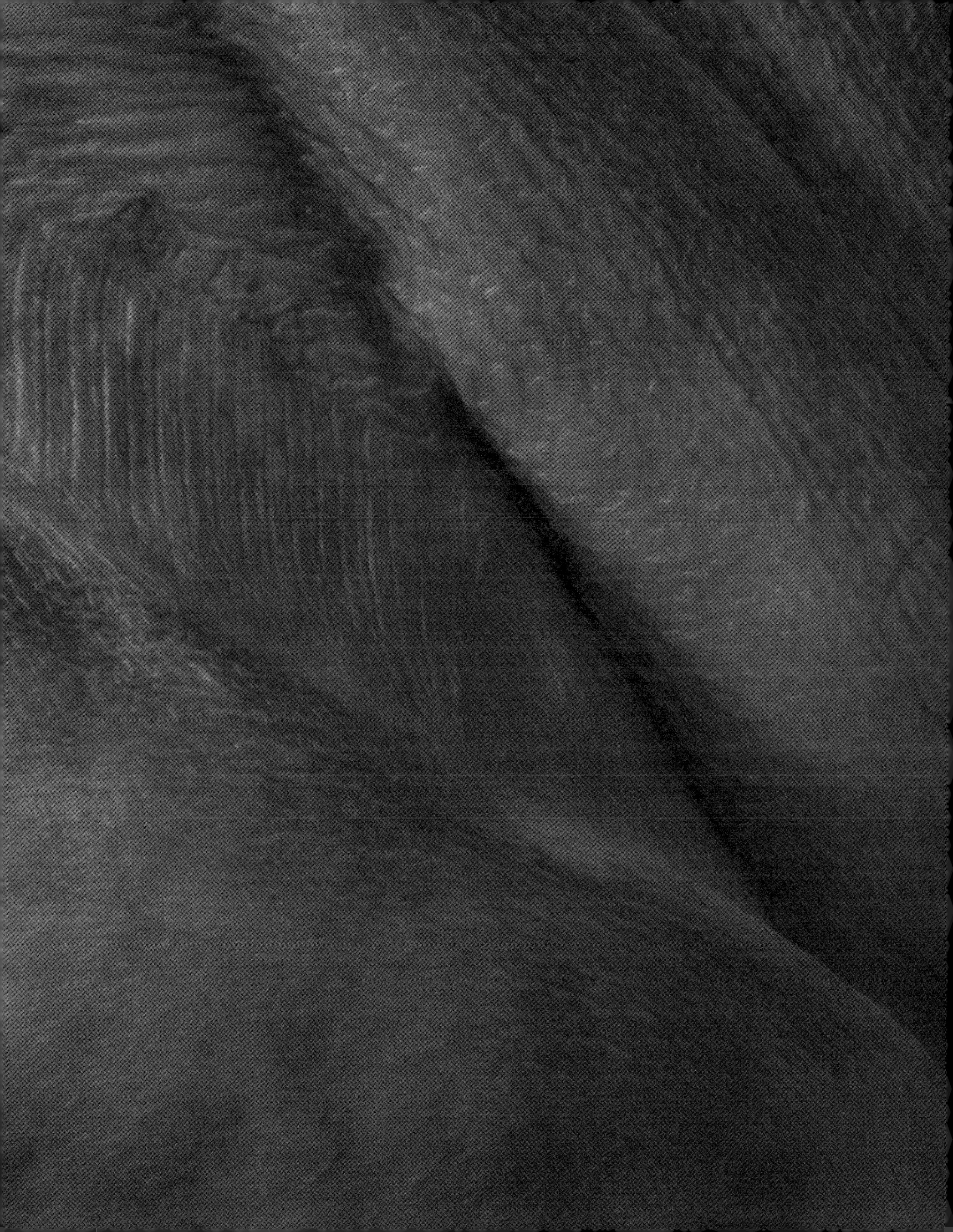

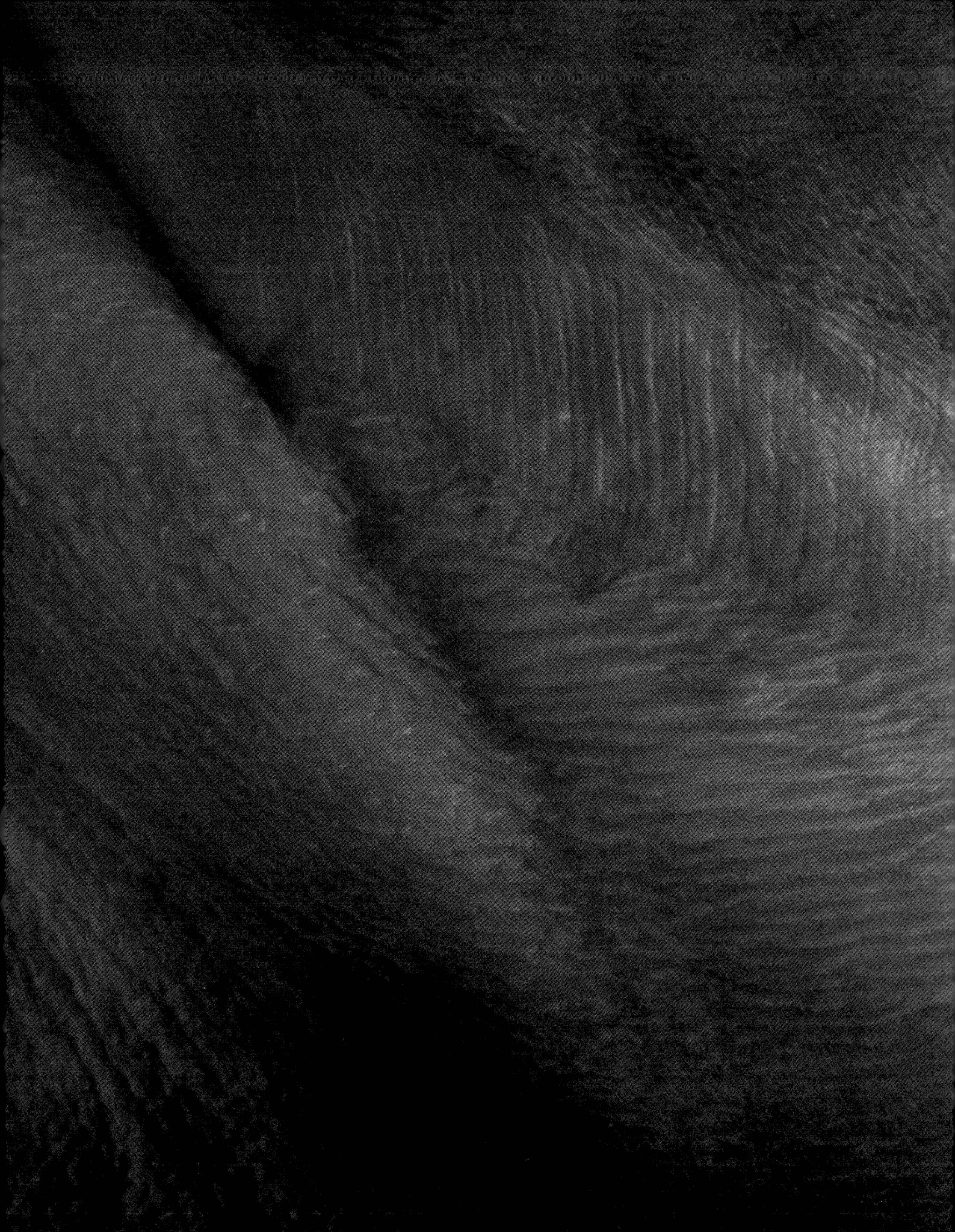

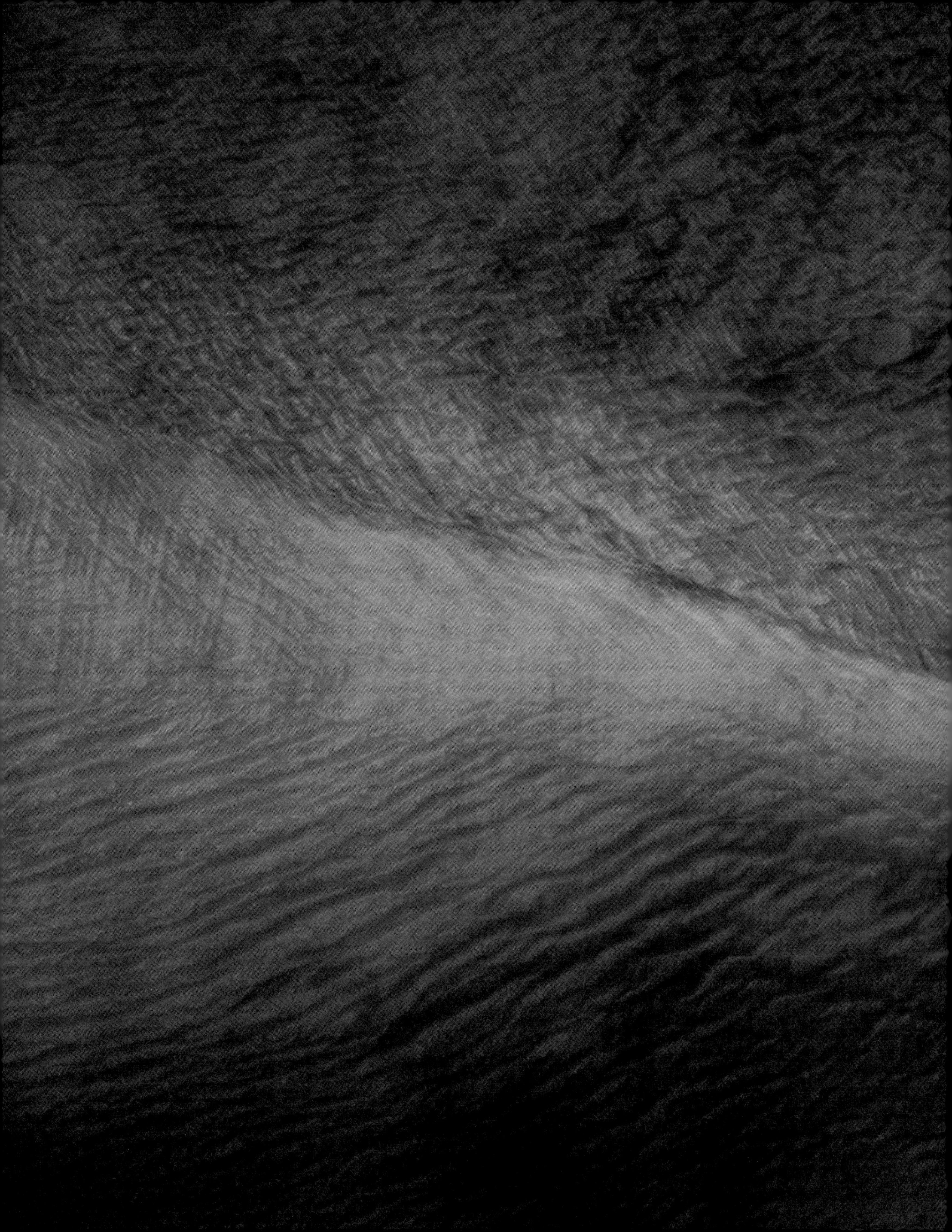

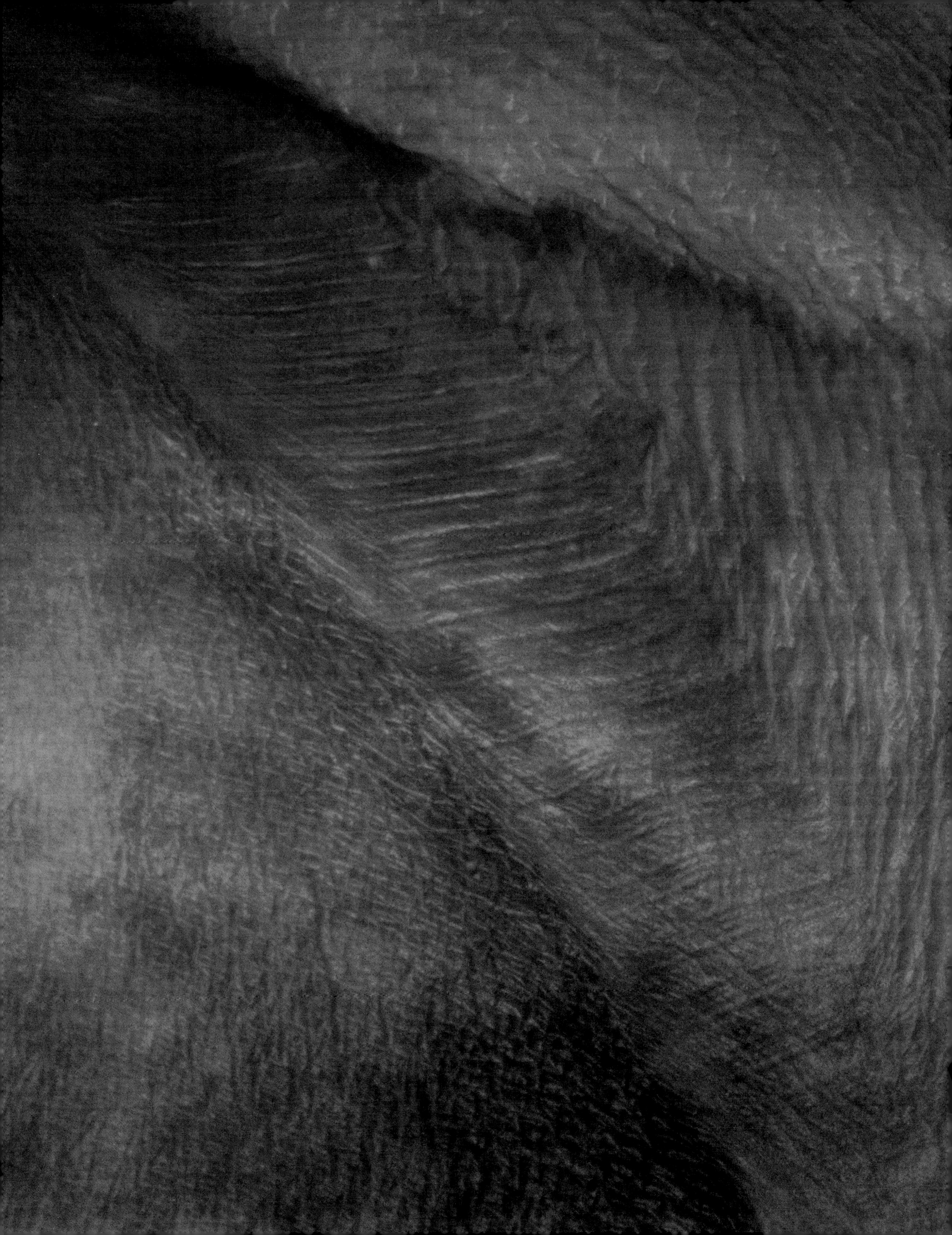

elle,

melle,

deg fo

rtelle

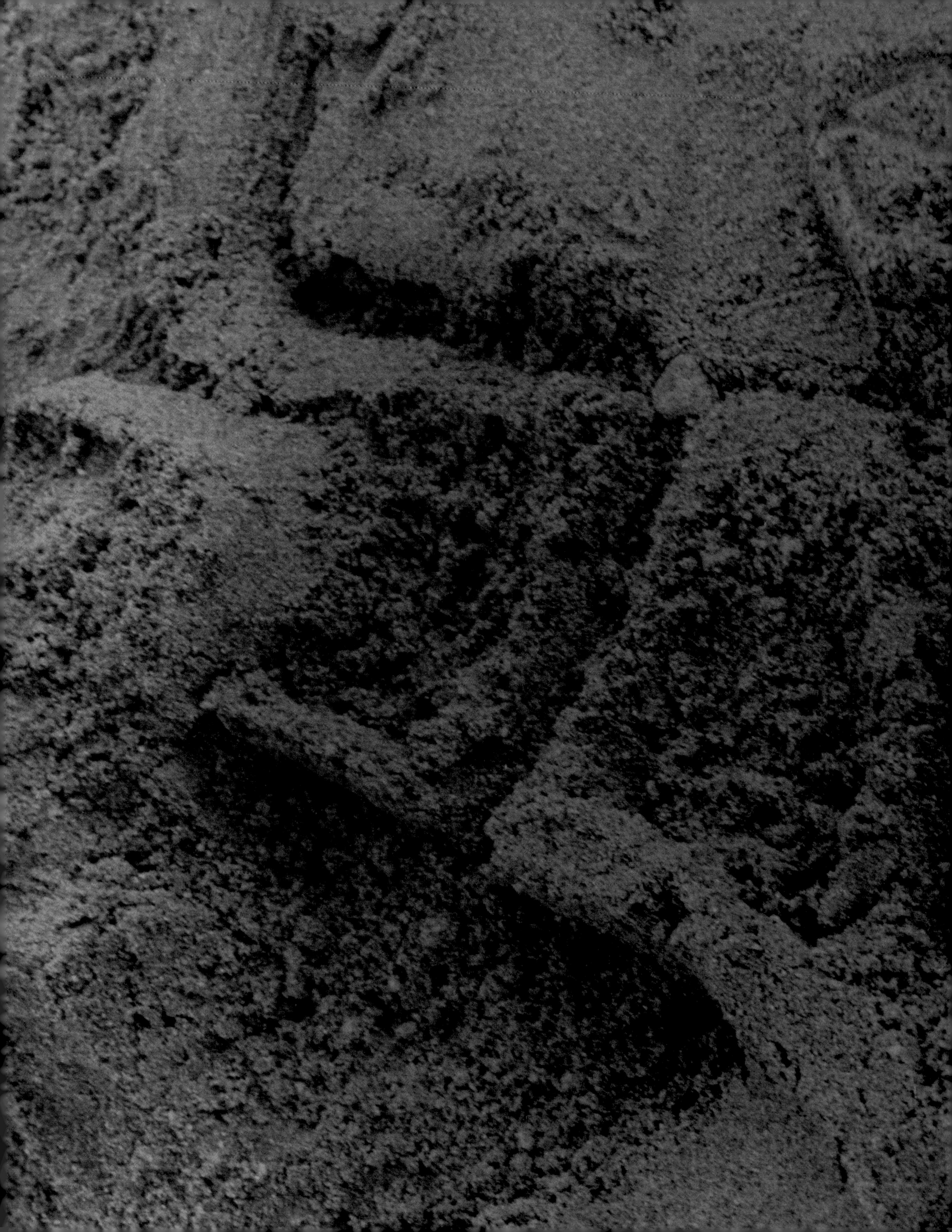

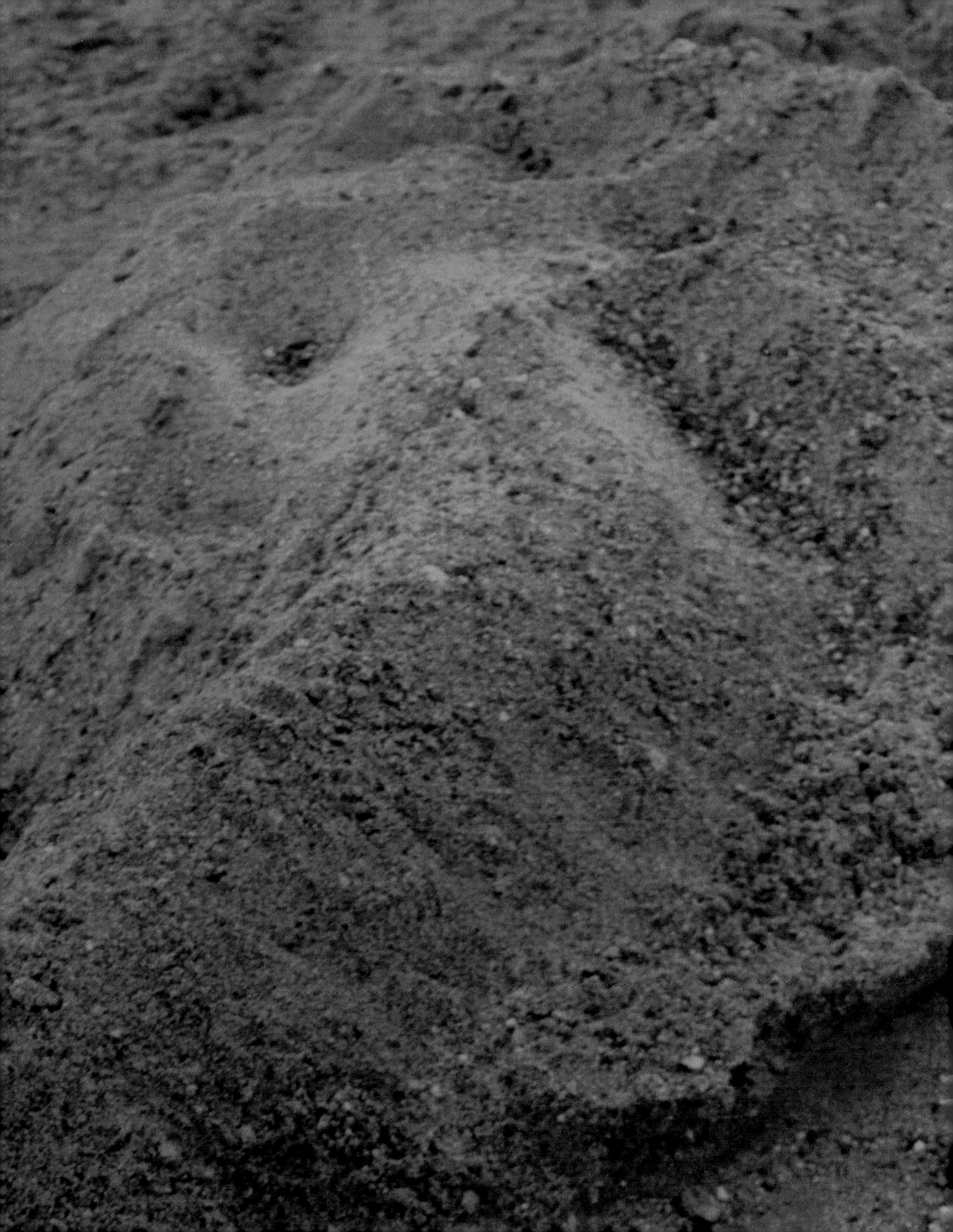

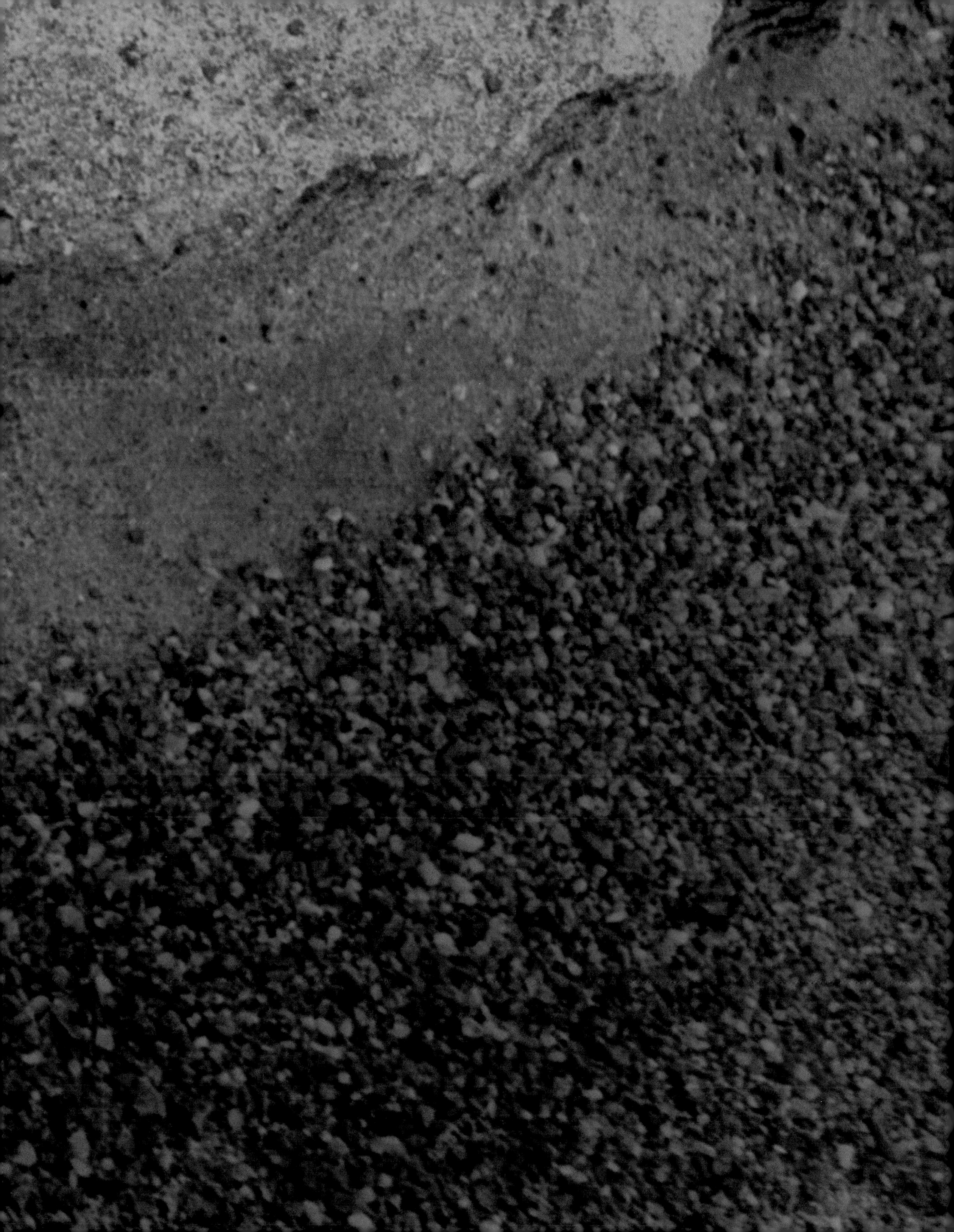

an

dam

des

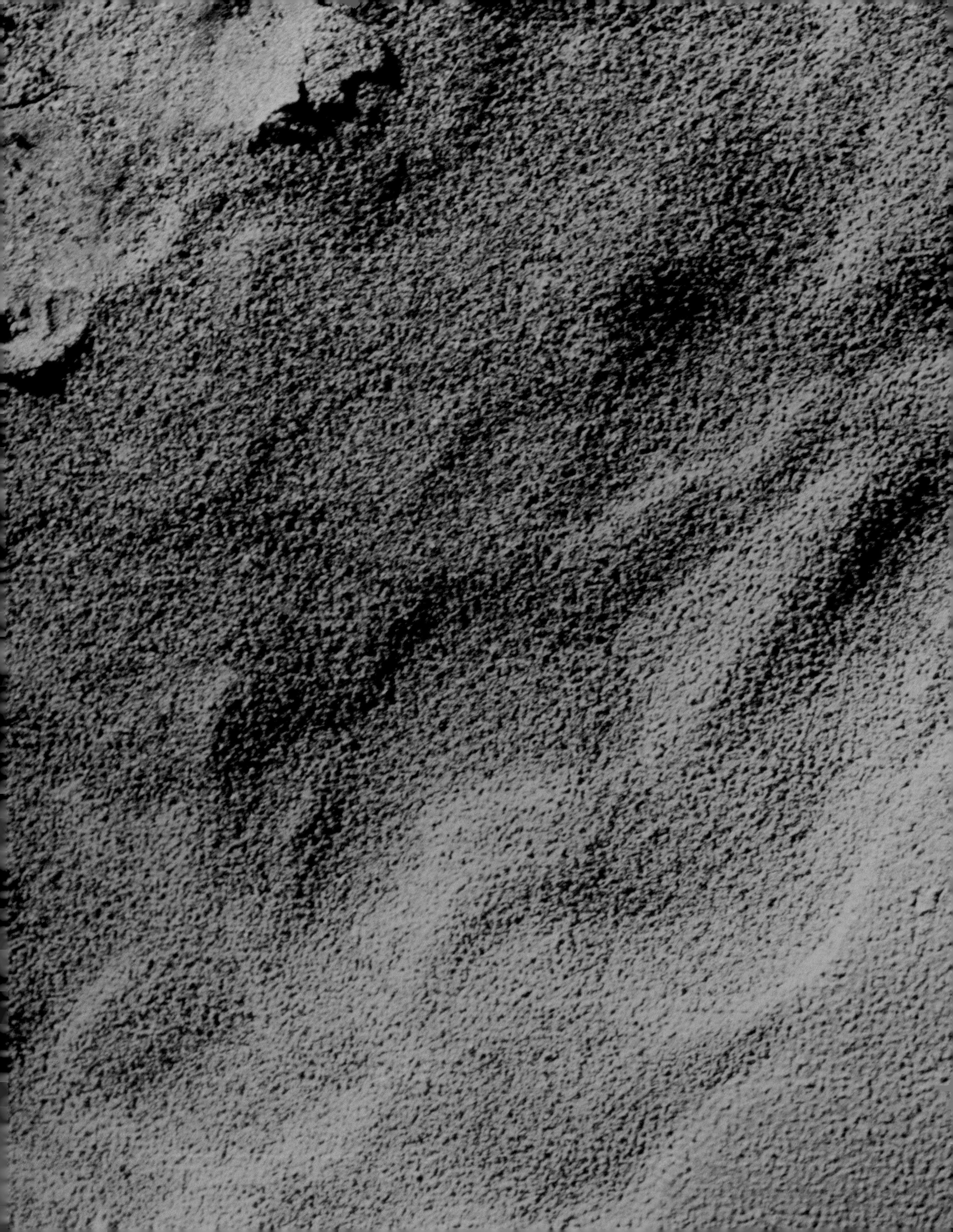

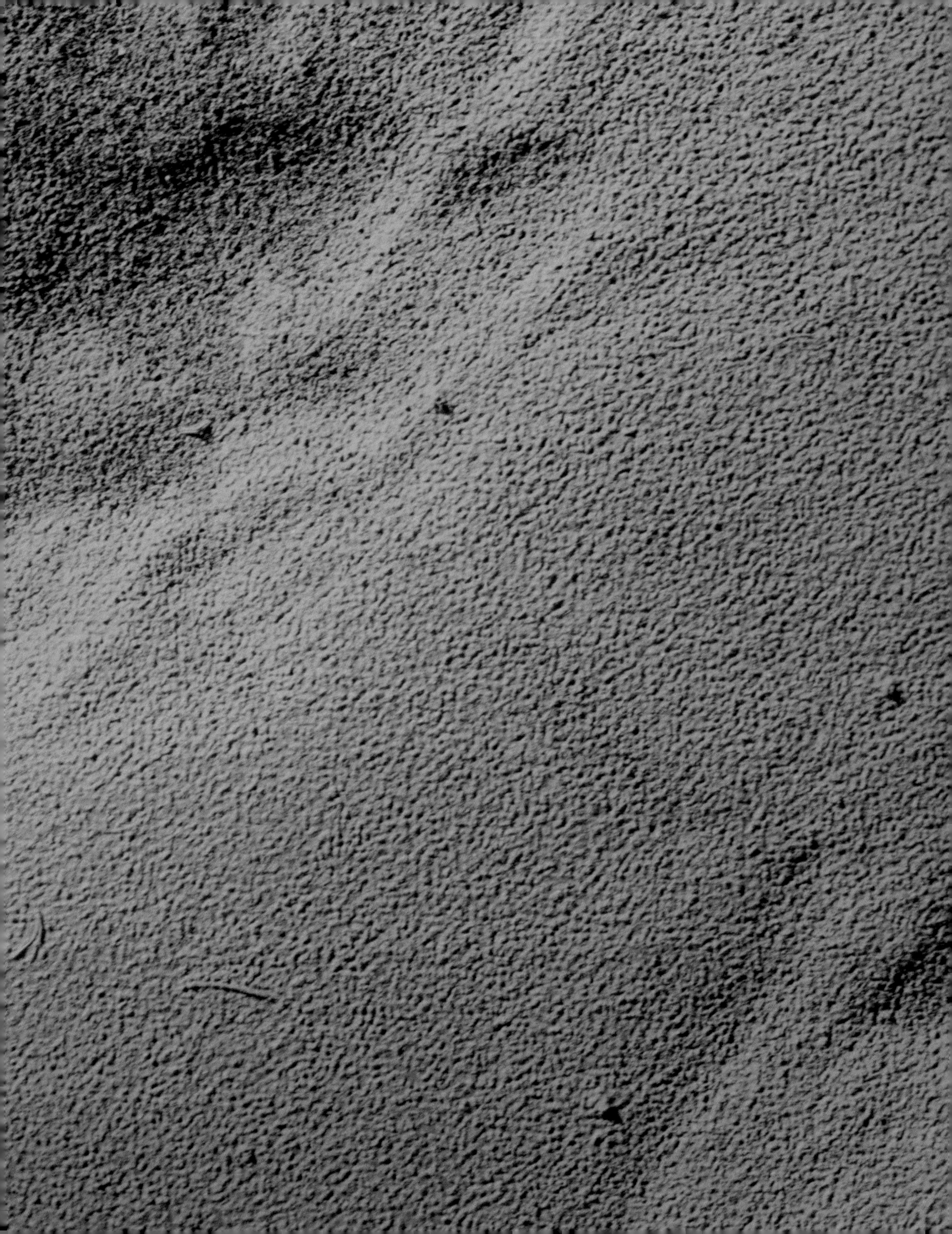

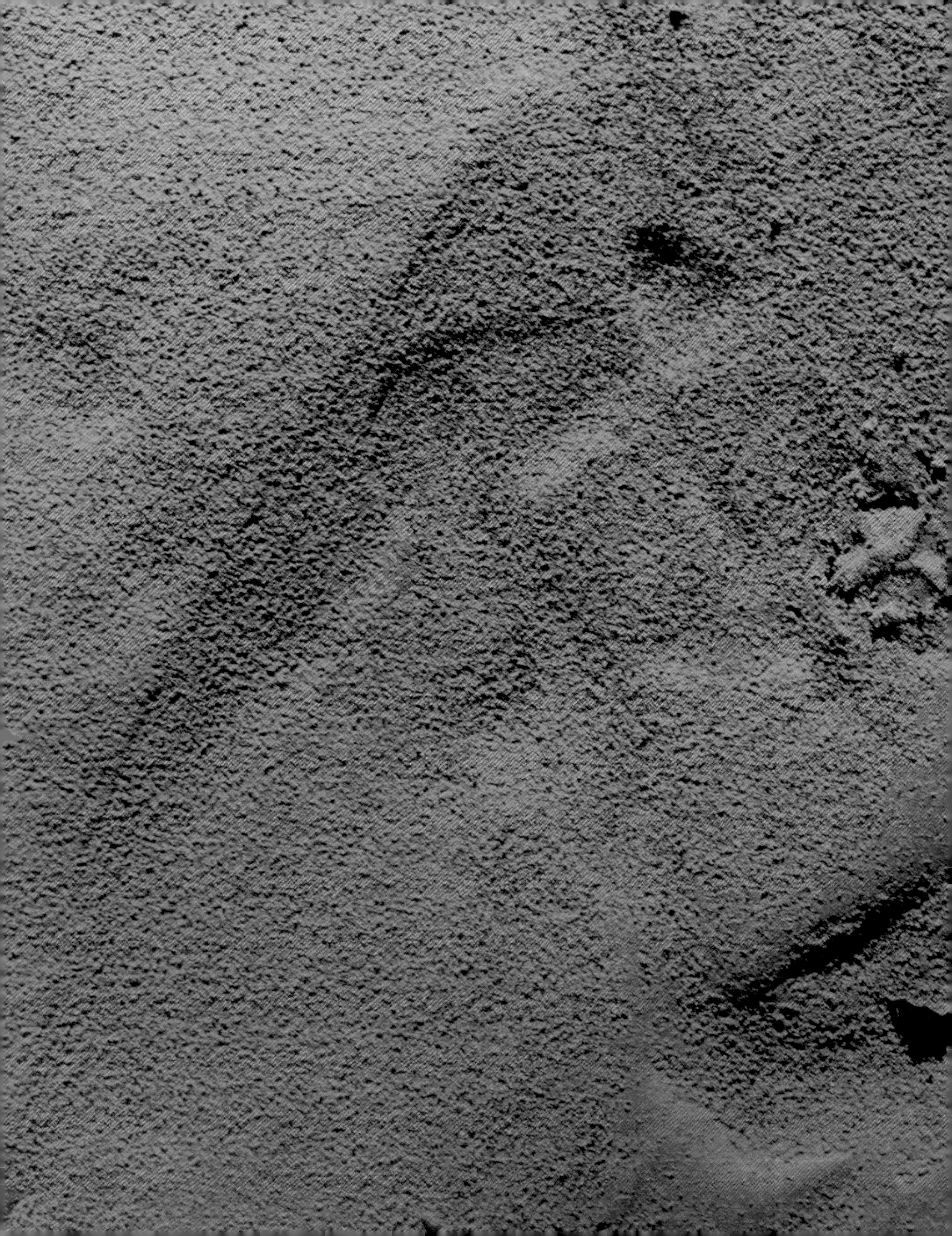

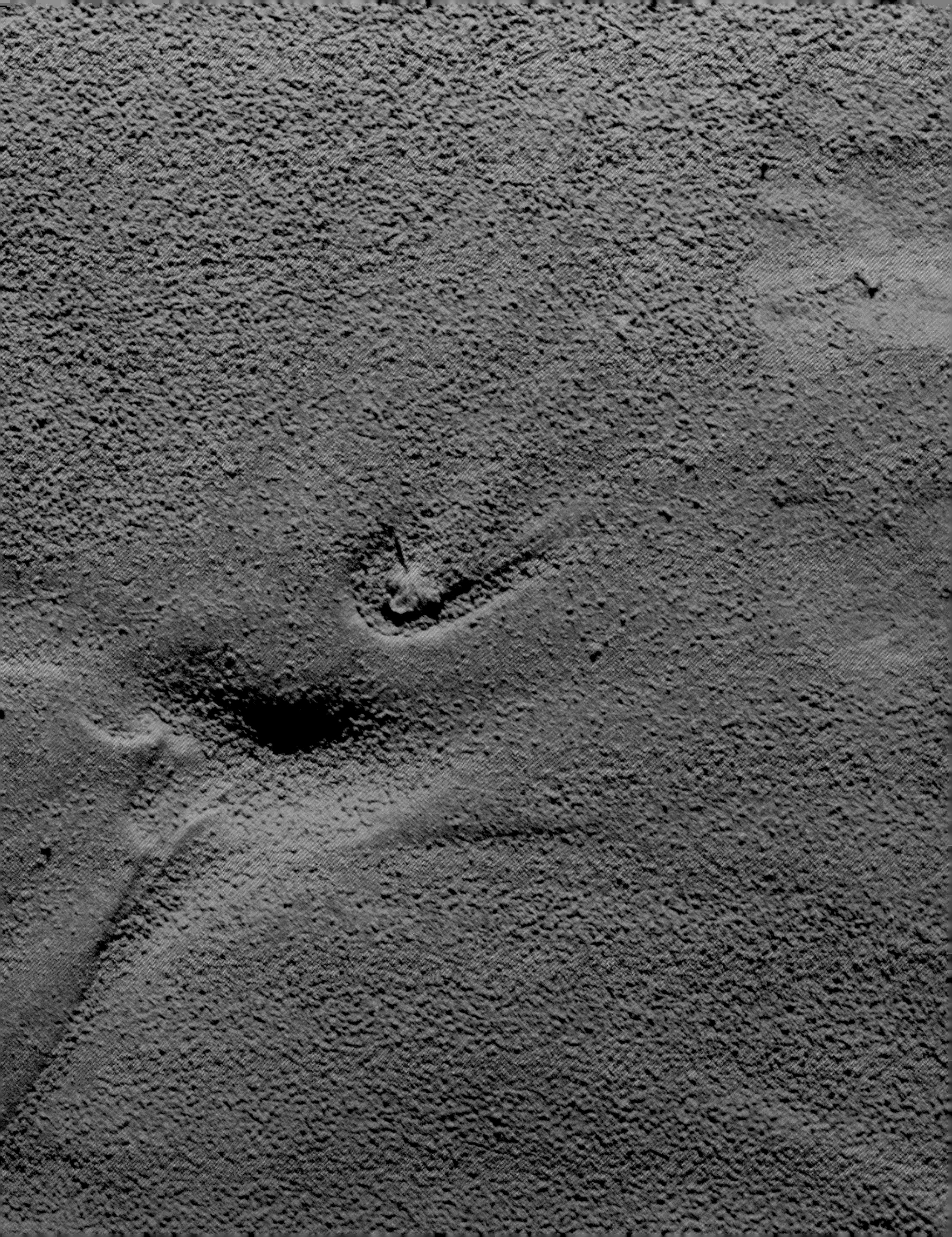

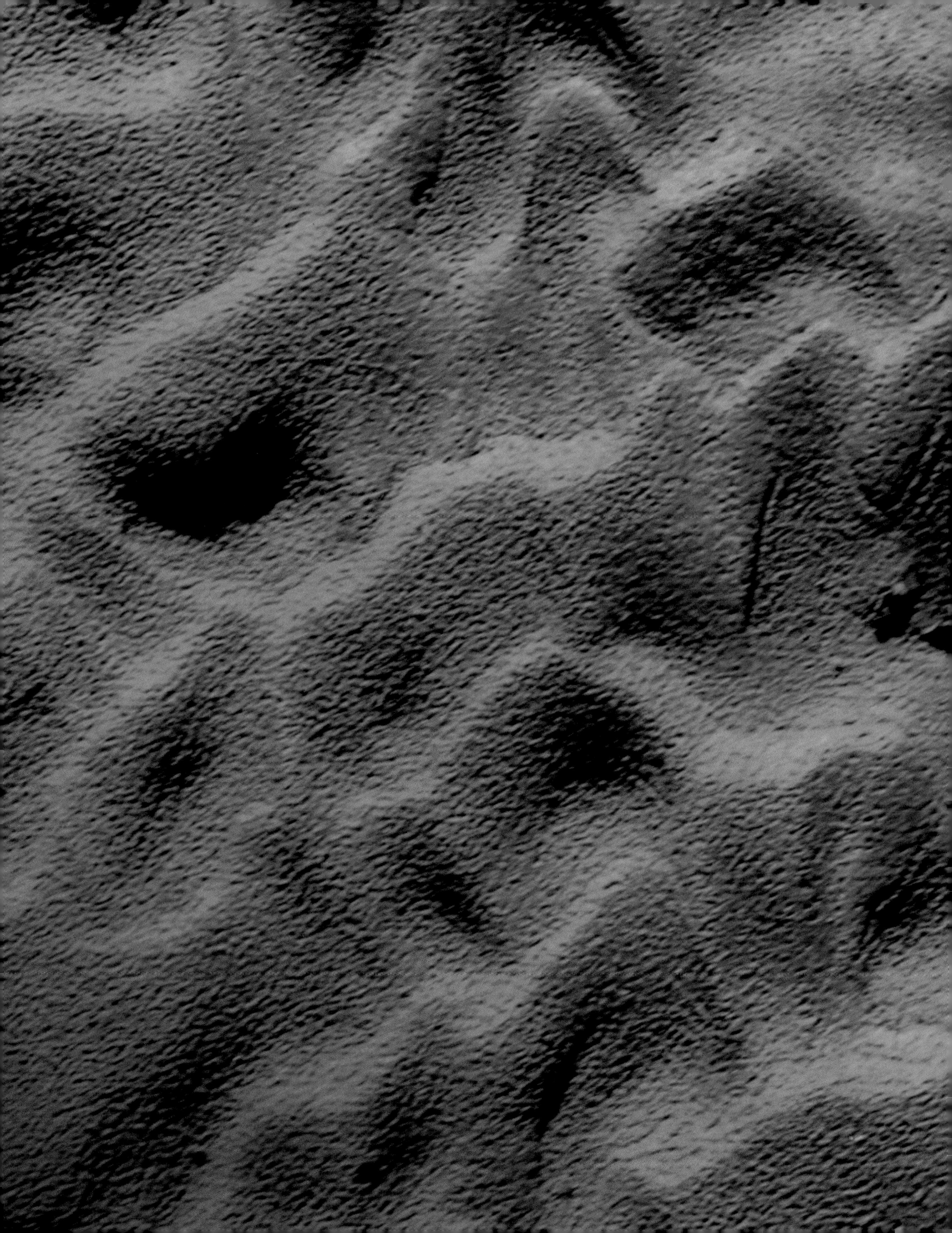

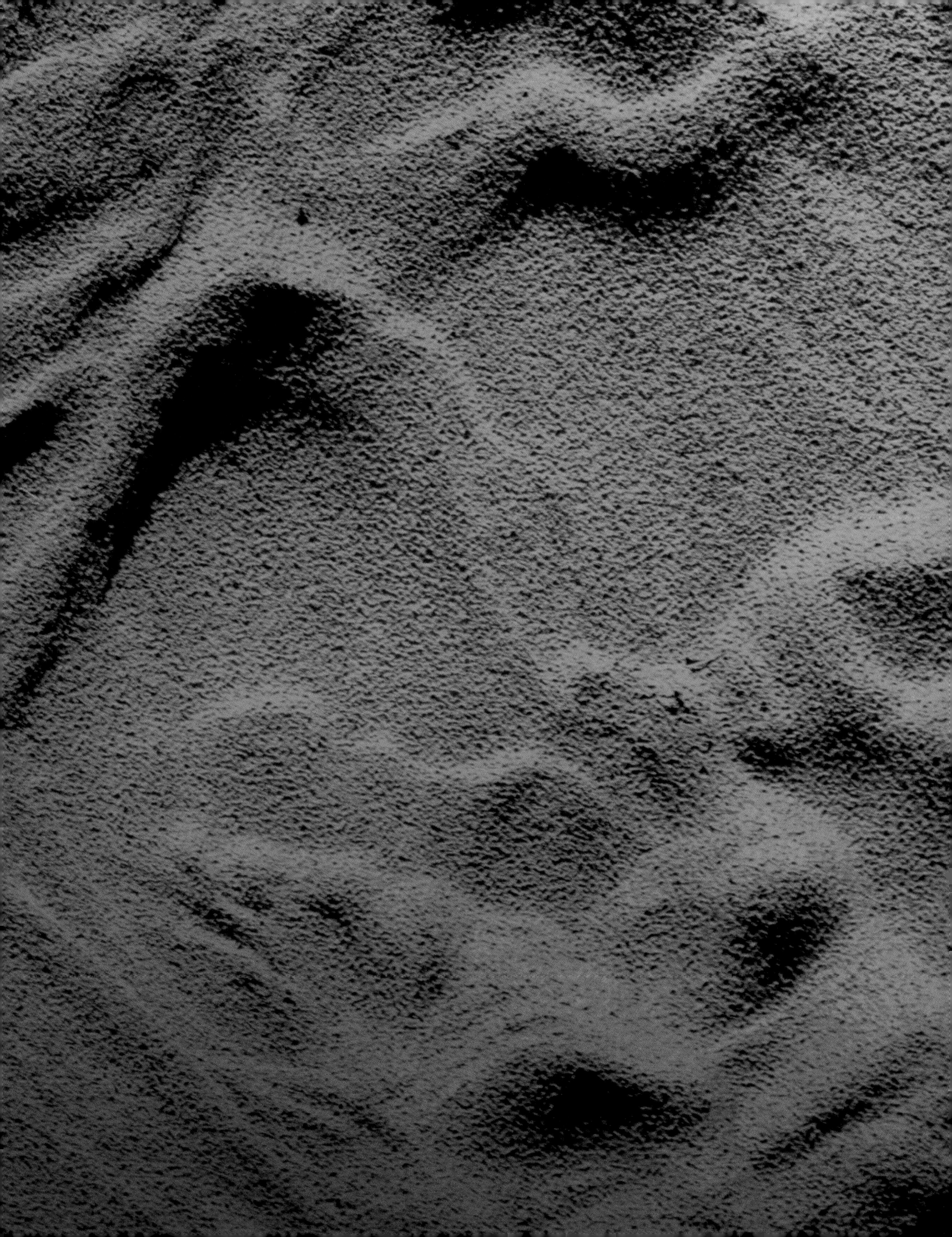

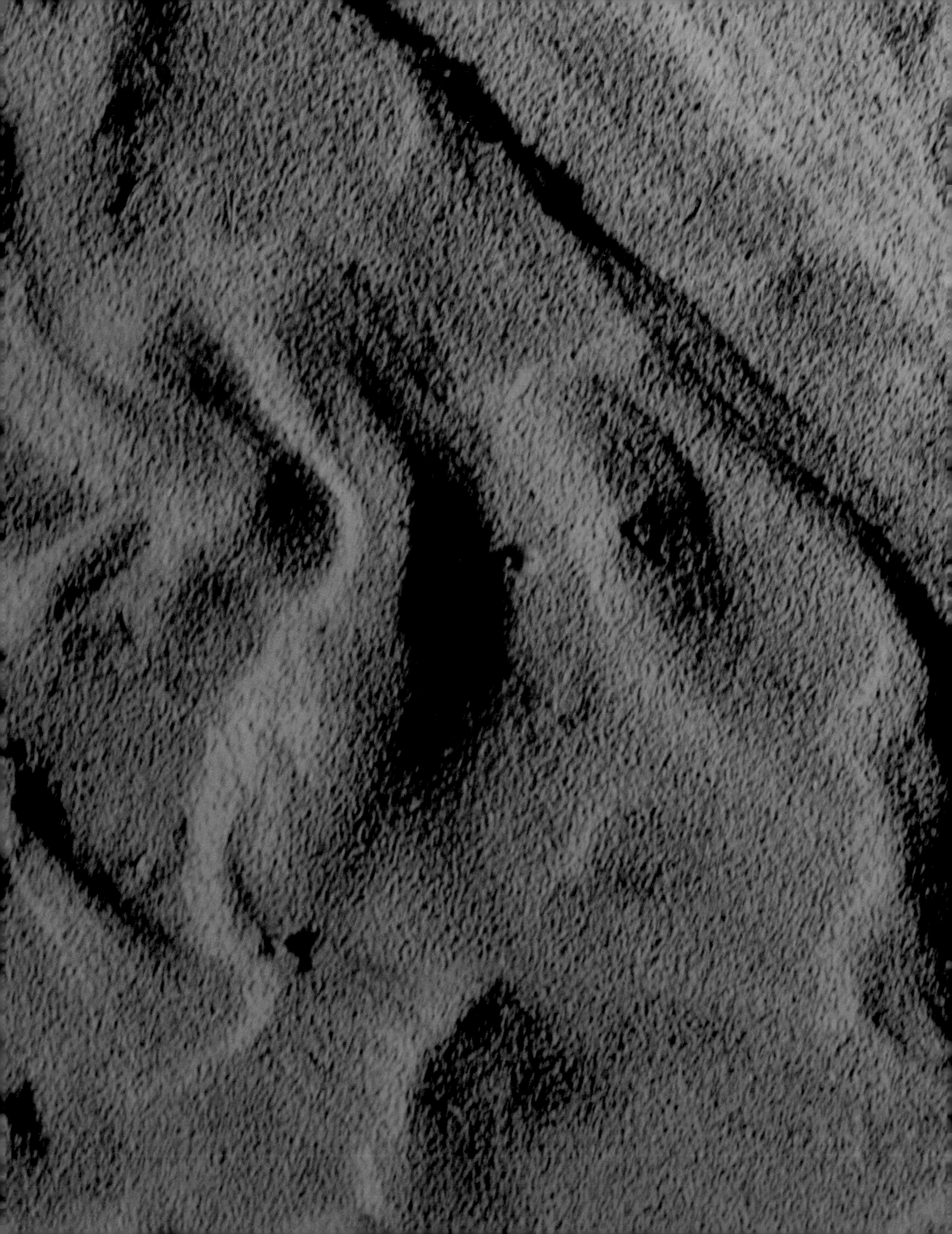

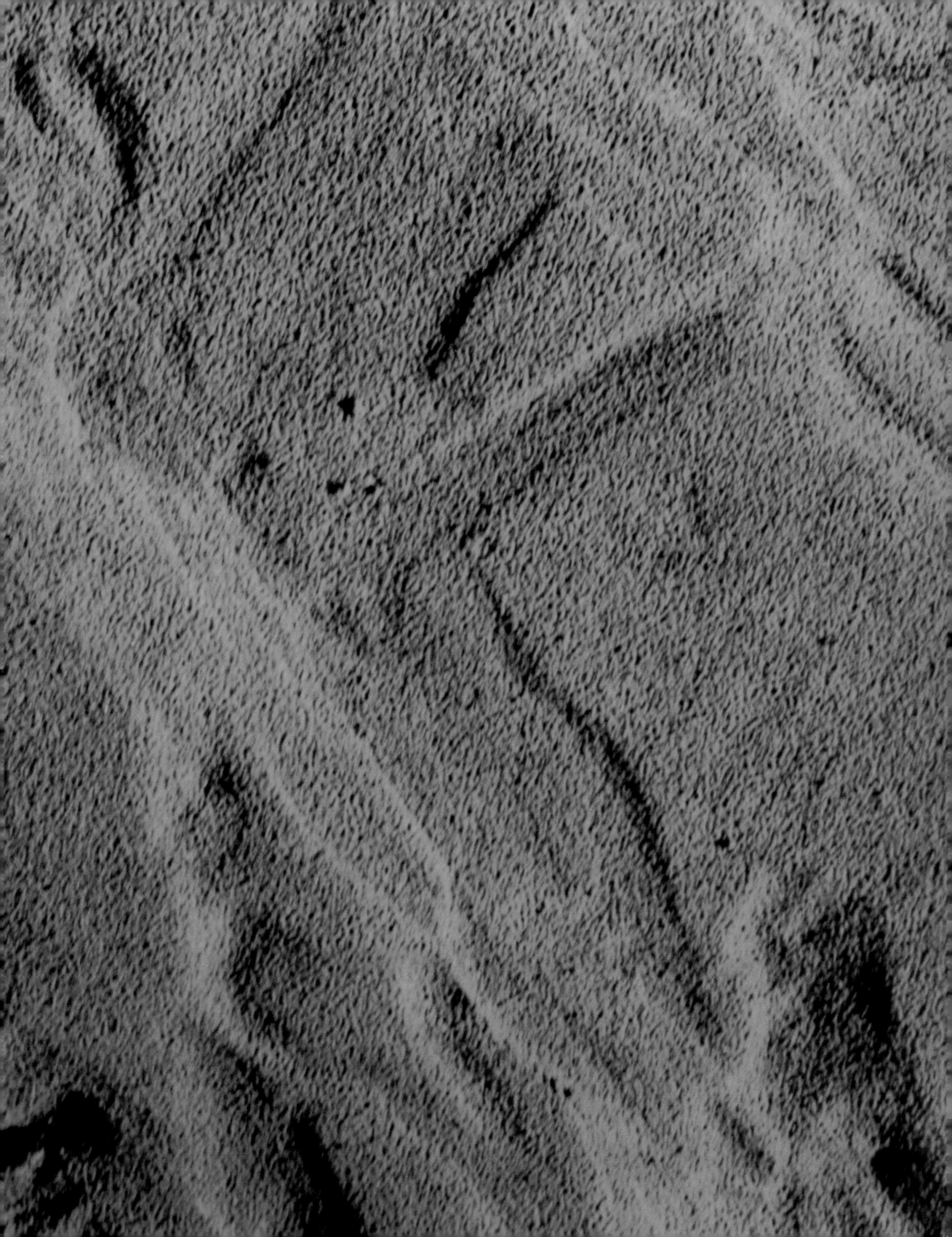

ene,

mene,

mink

mank

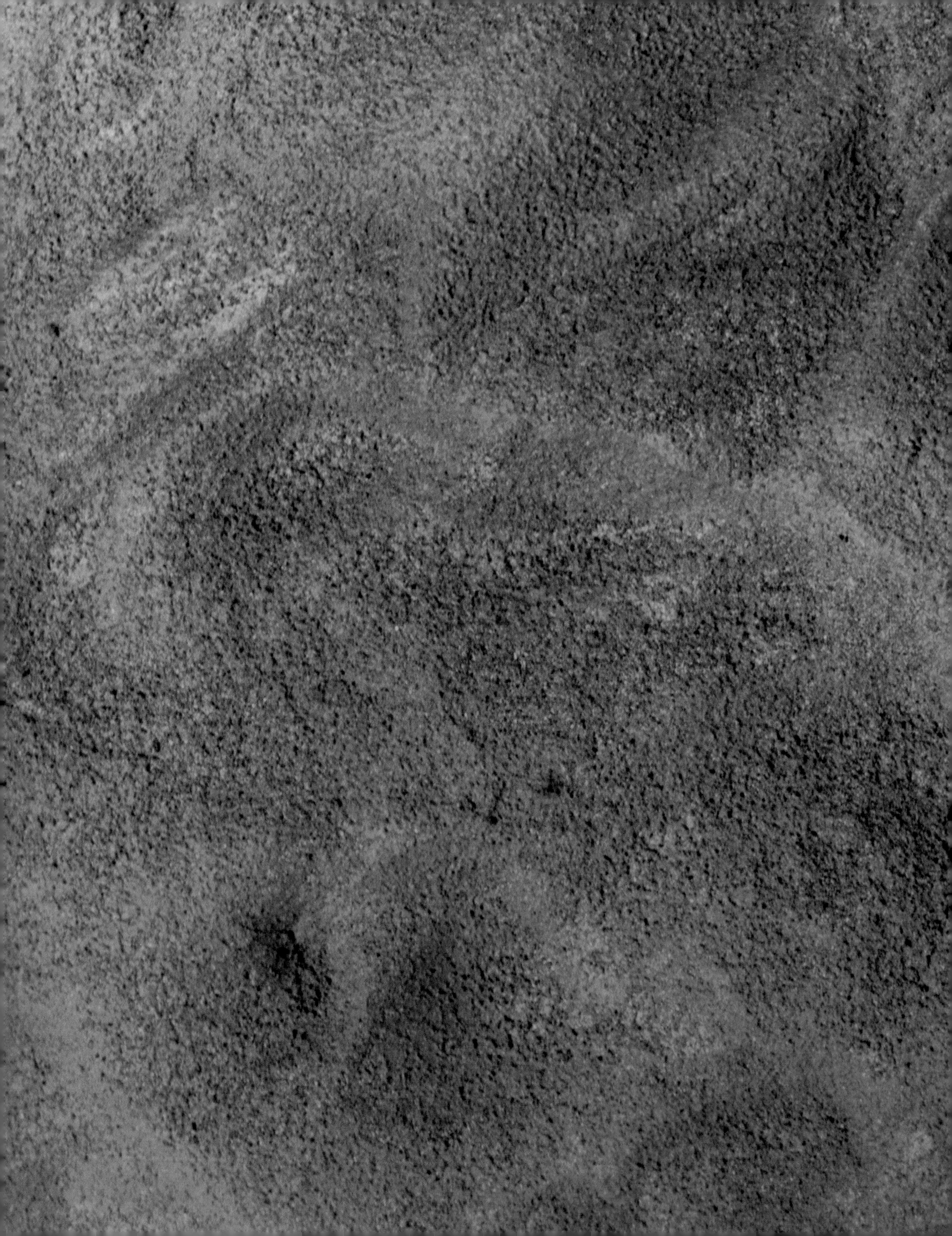

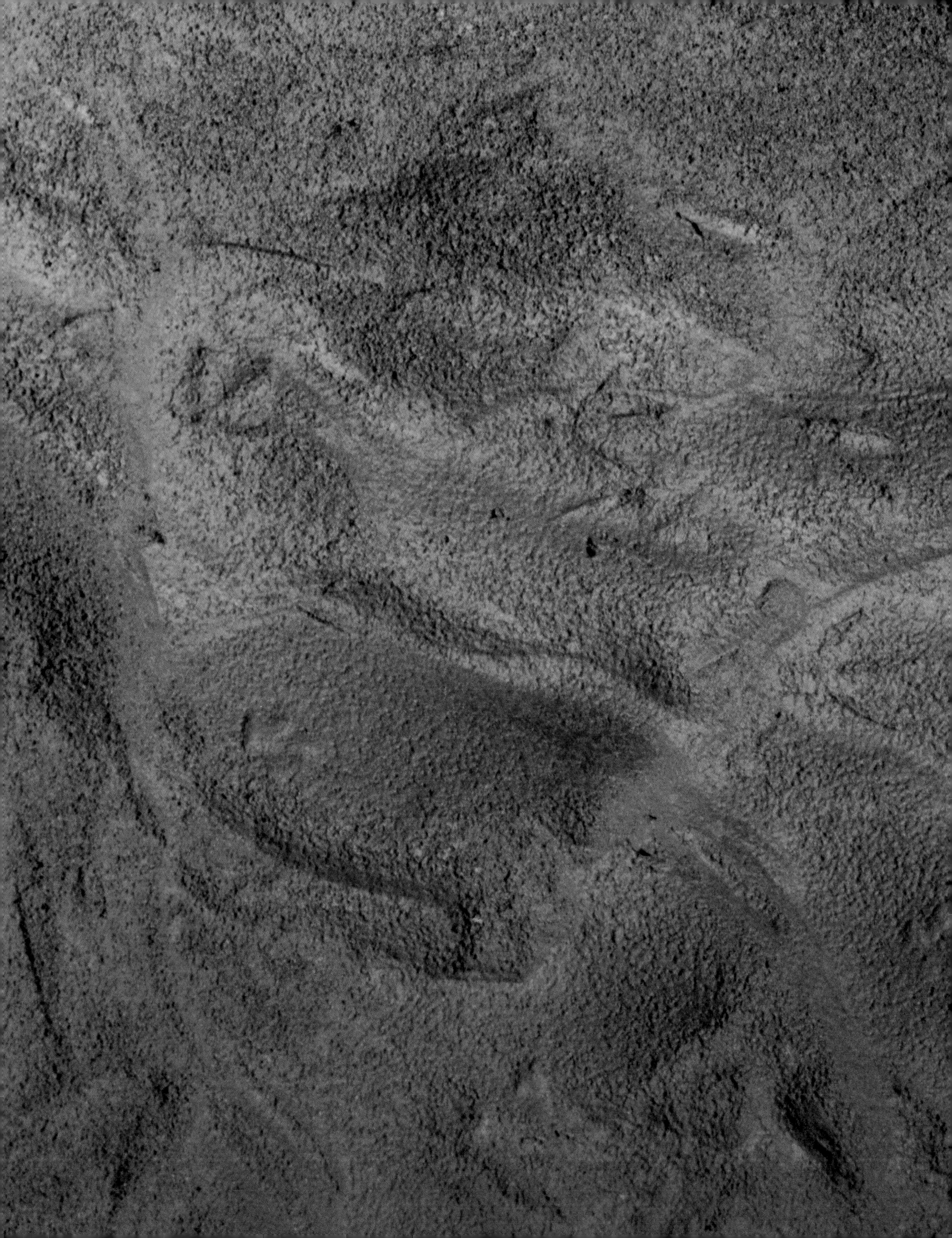

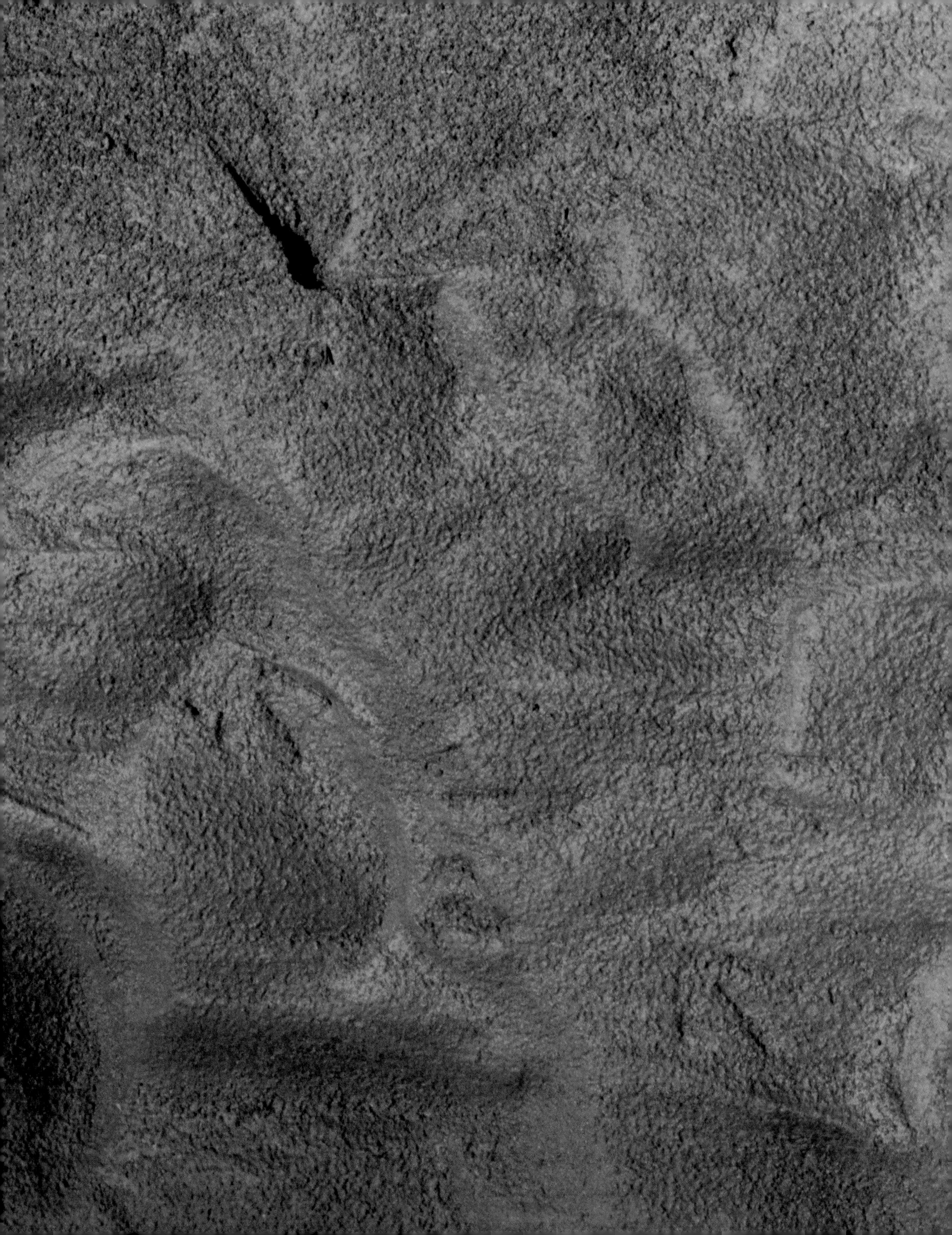

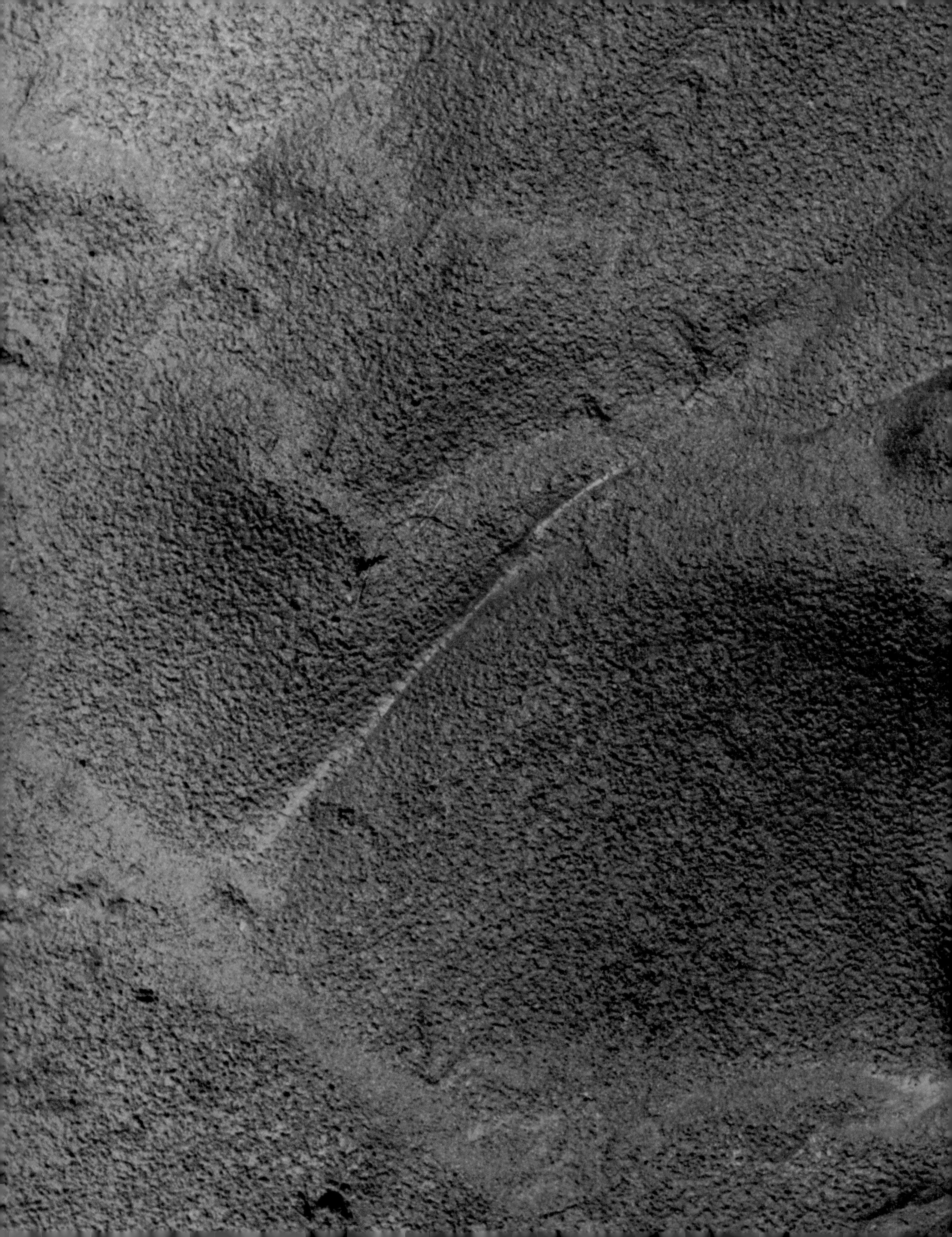

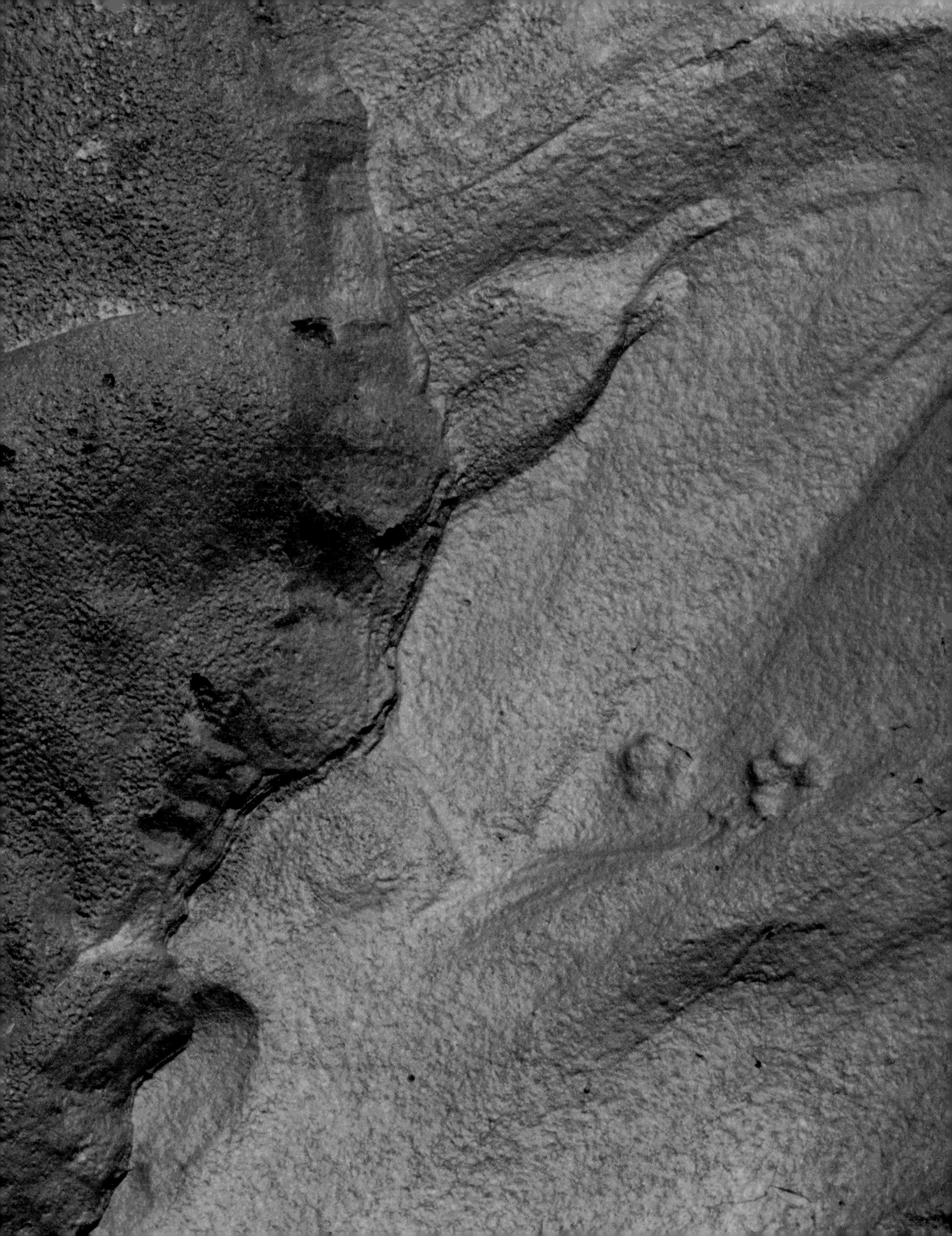

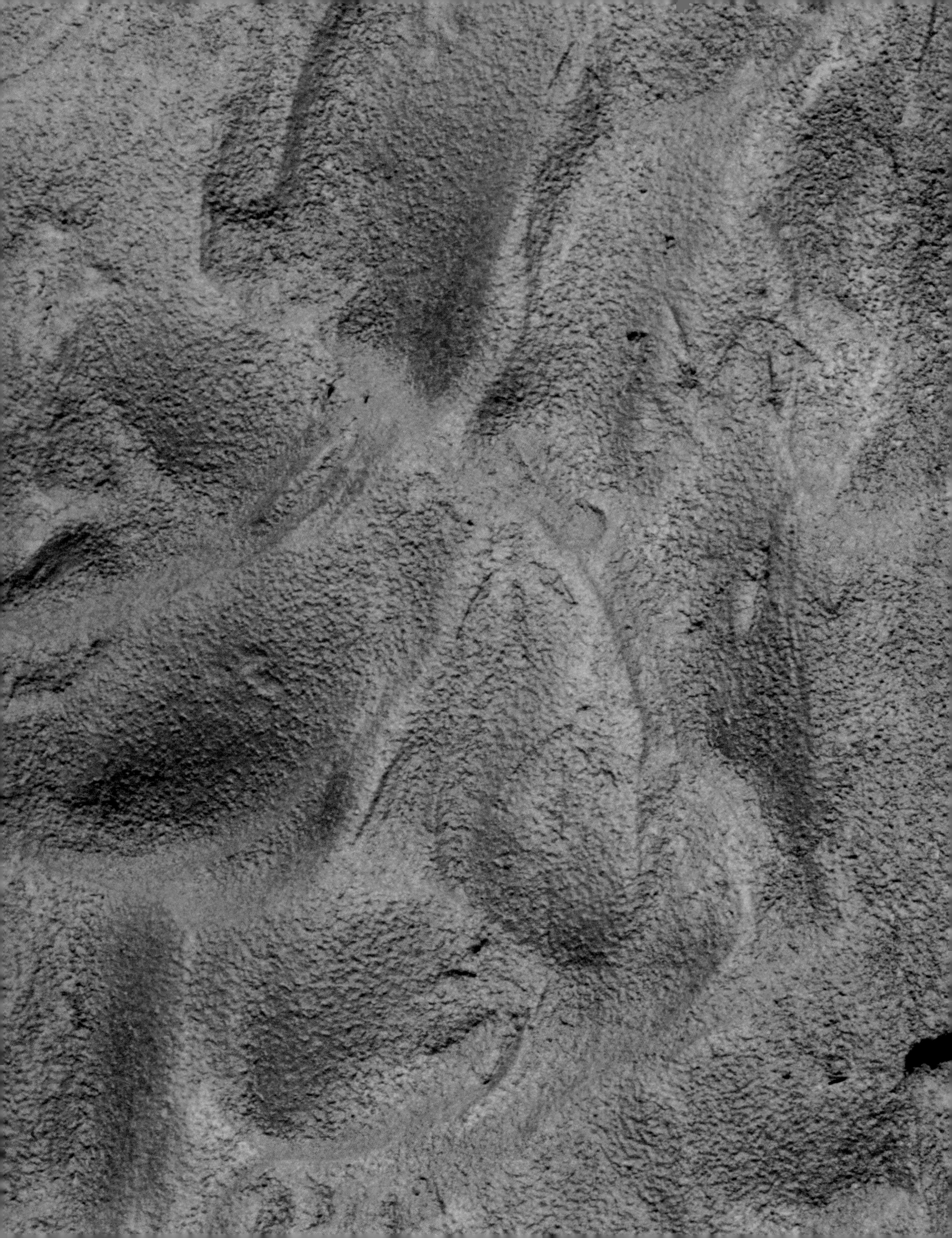

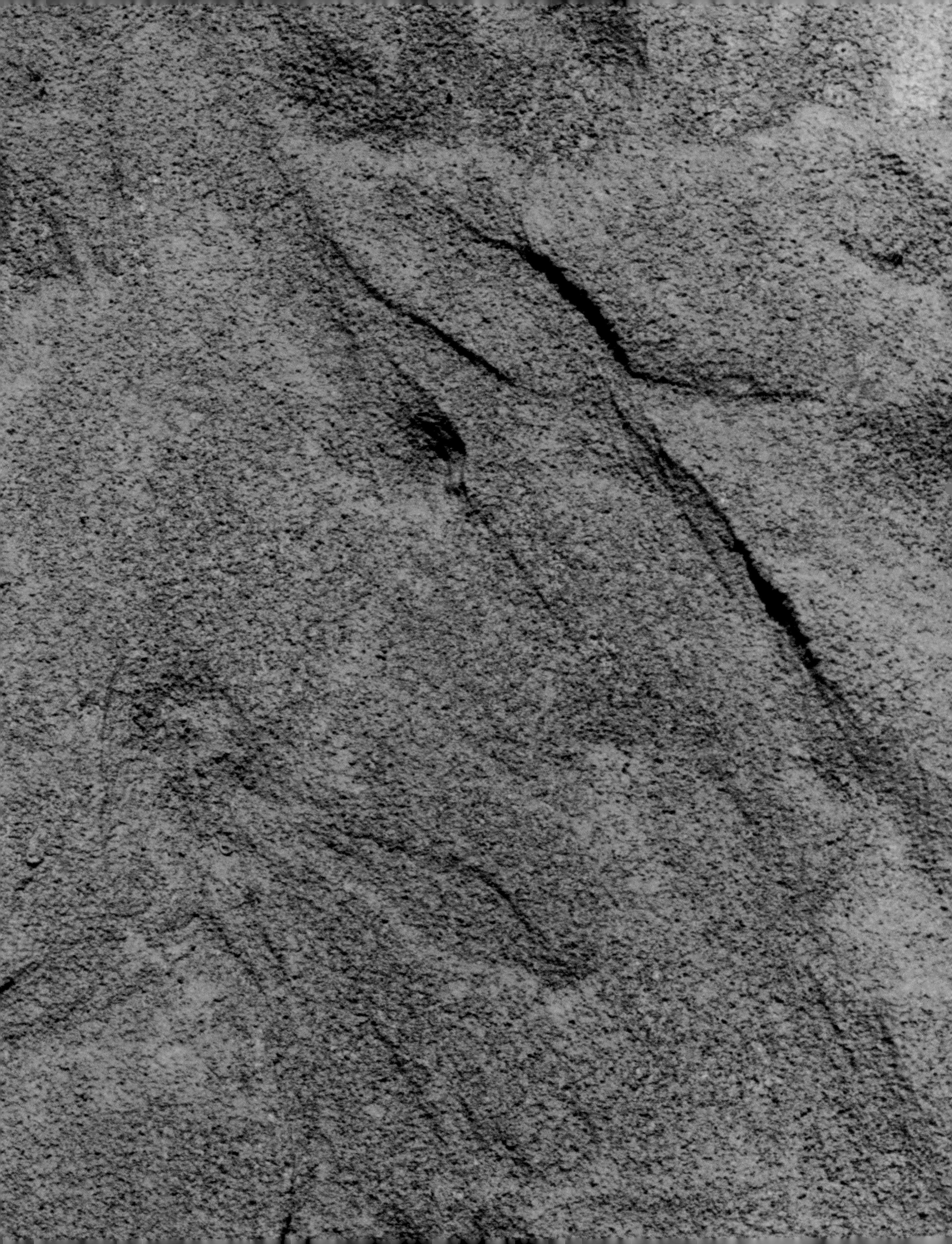

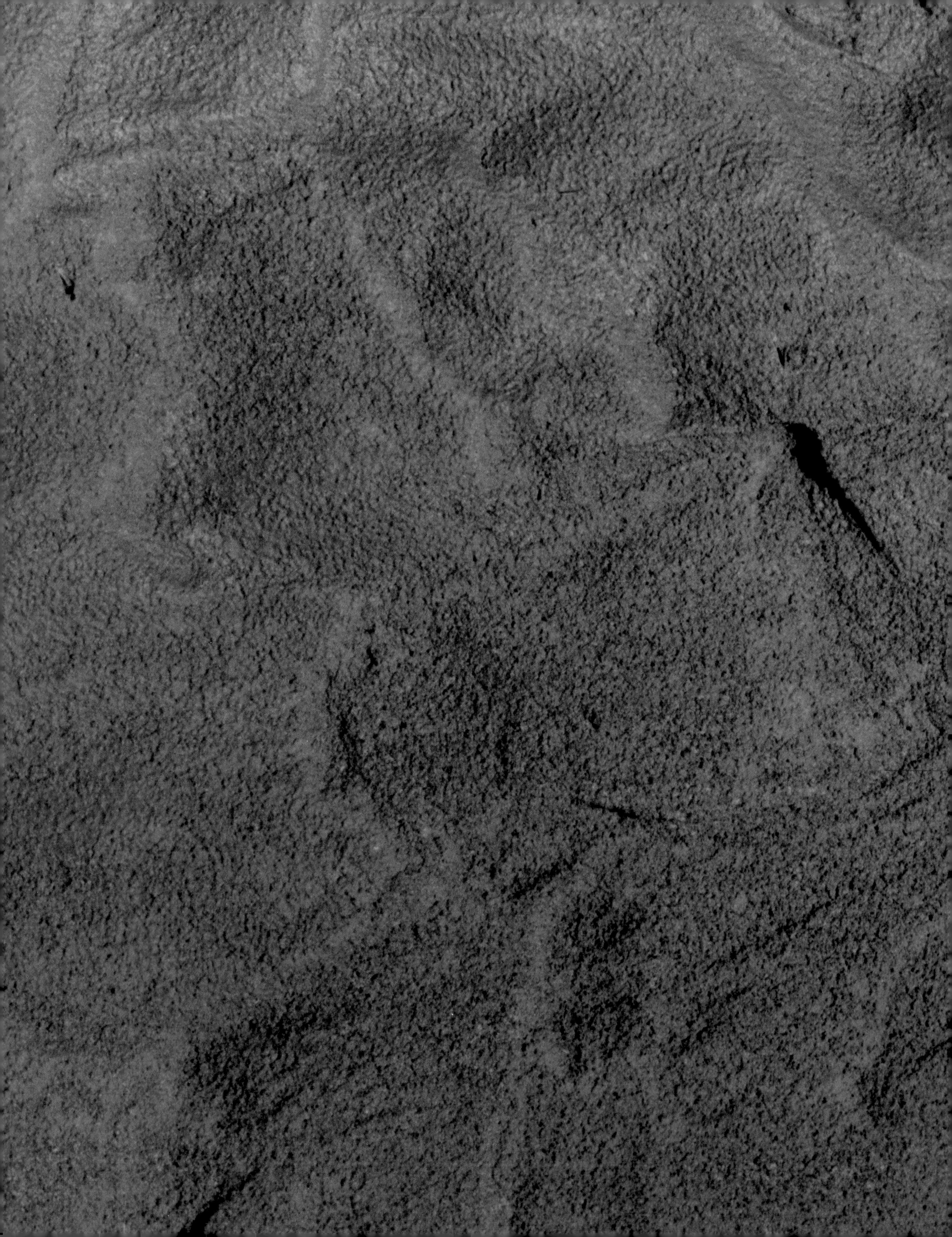

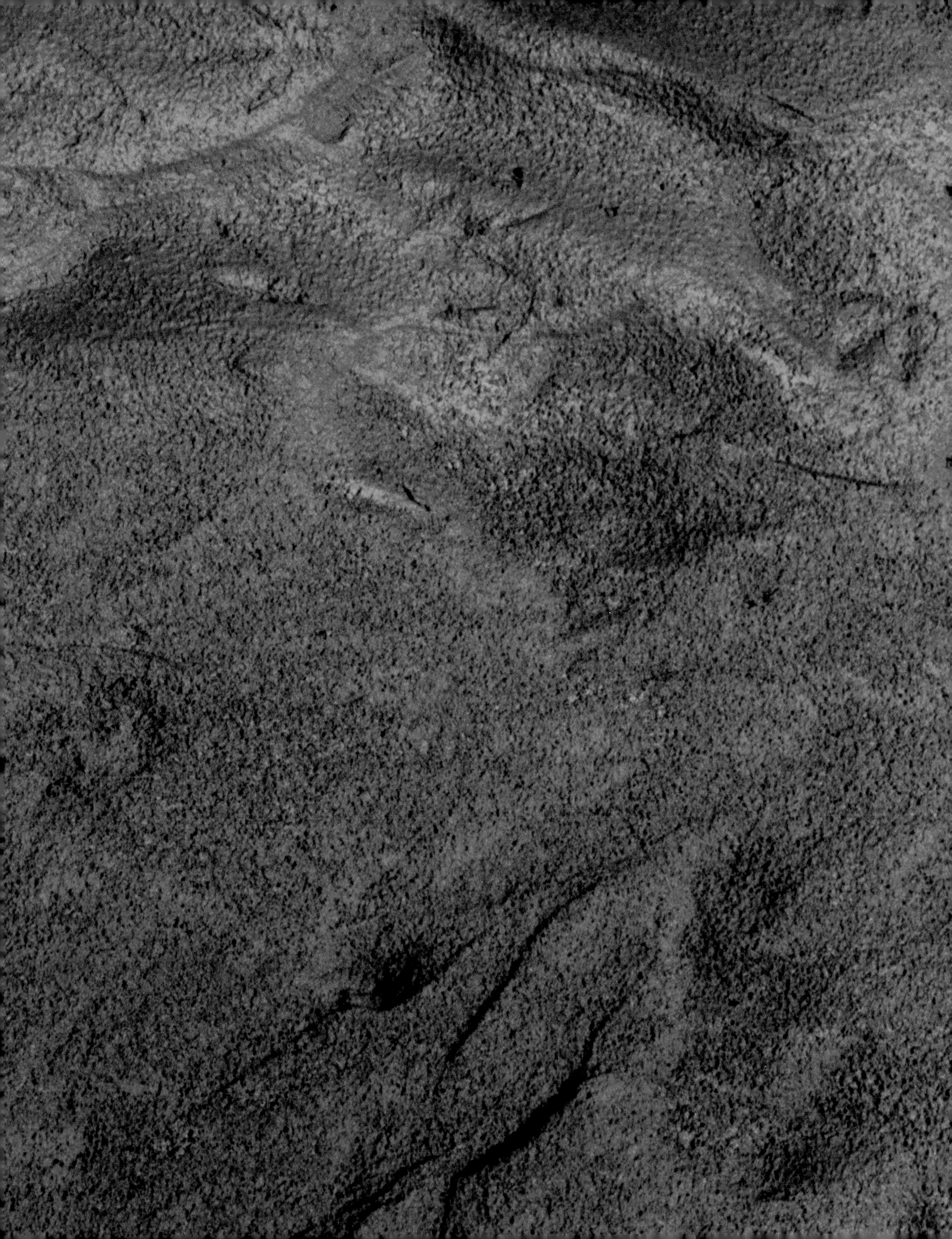

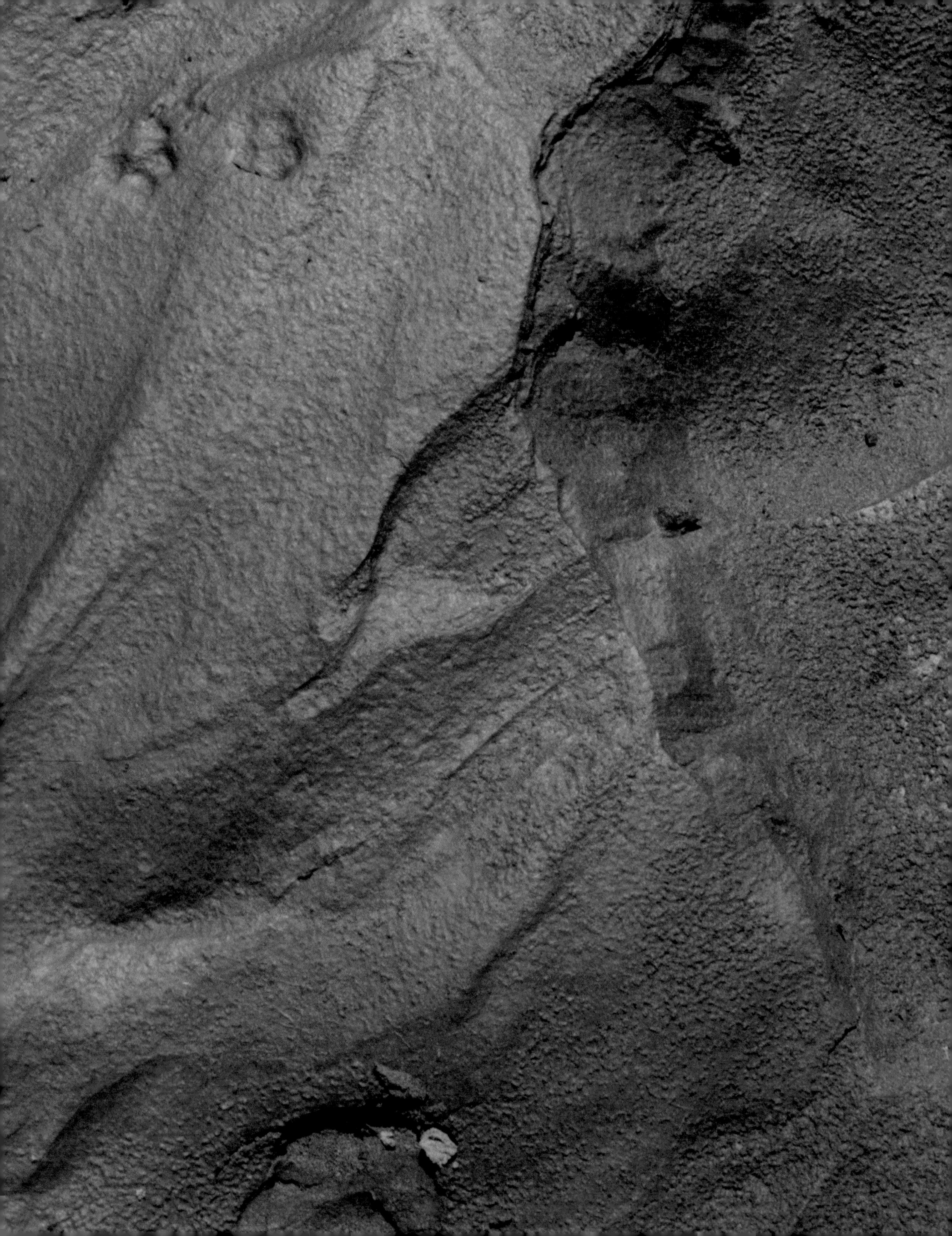

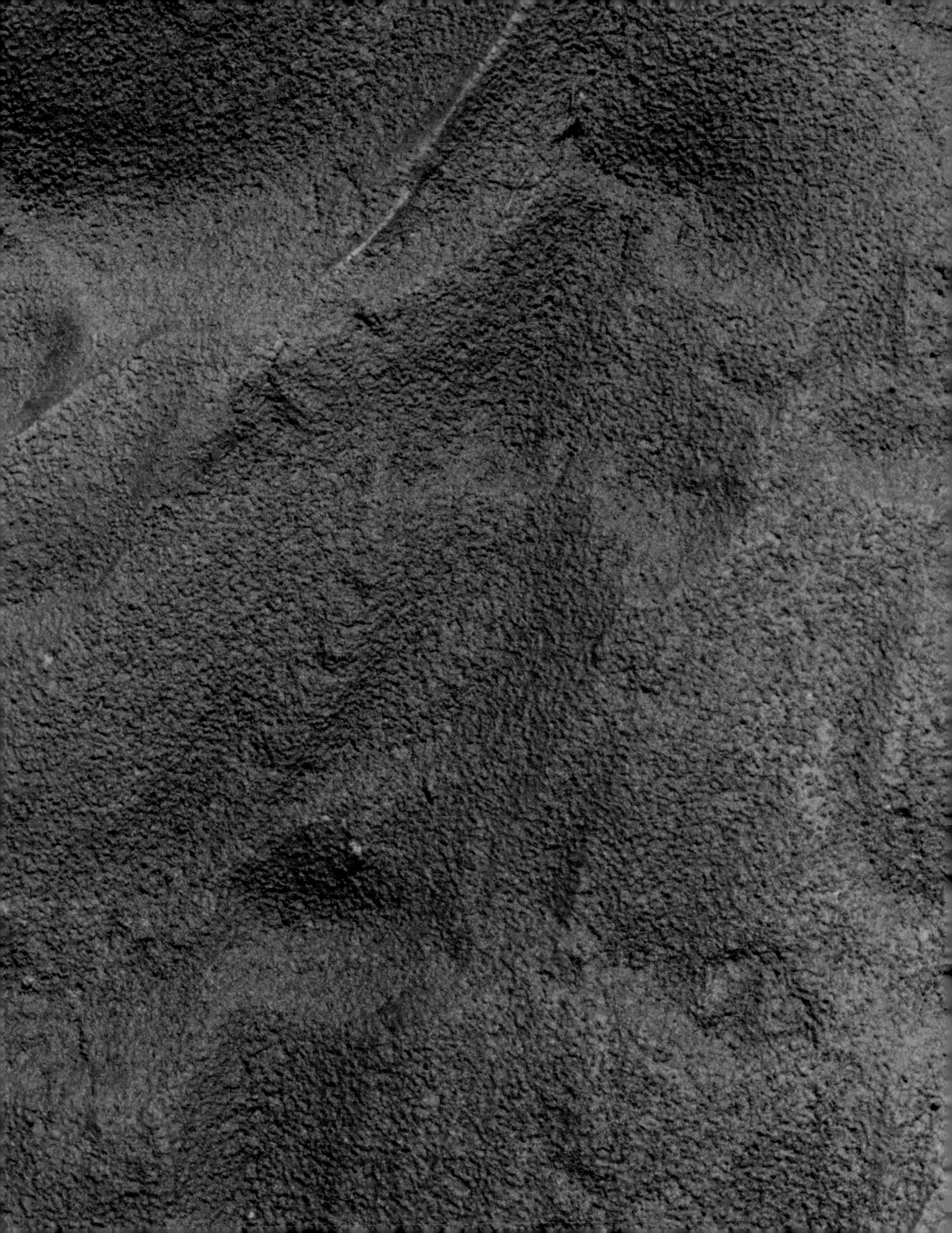

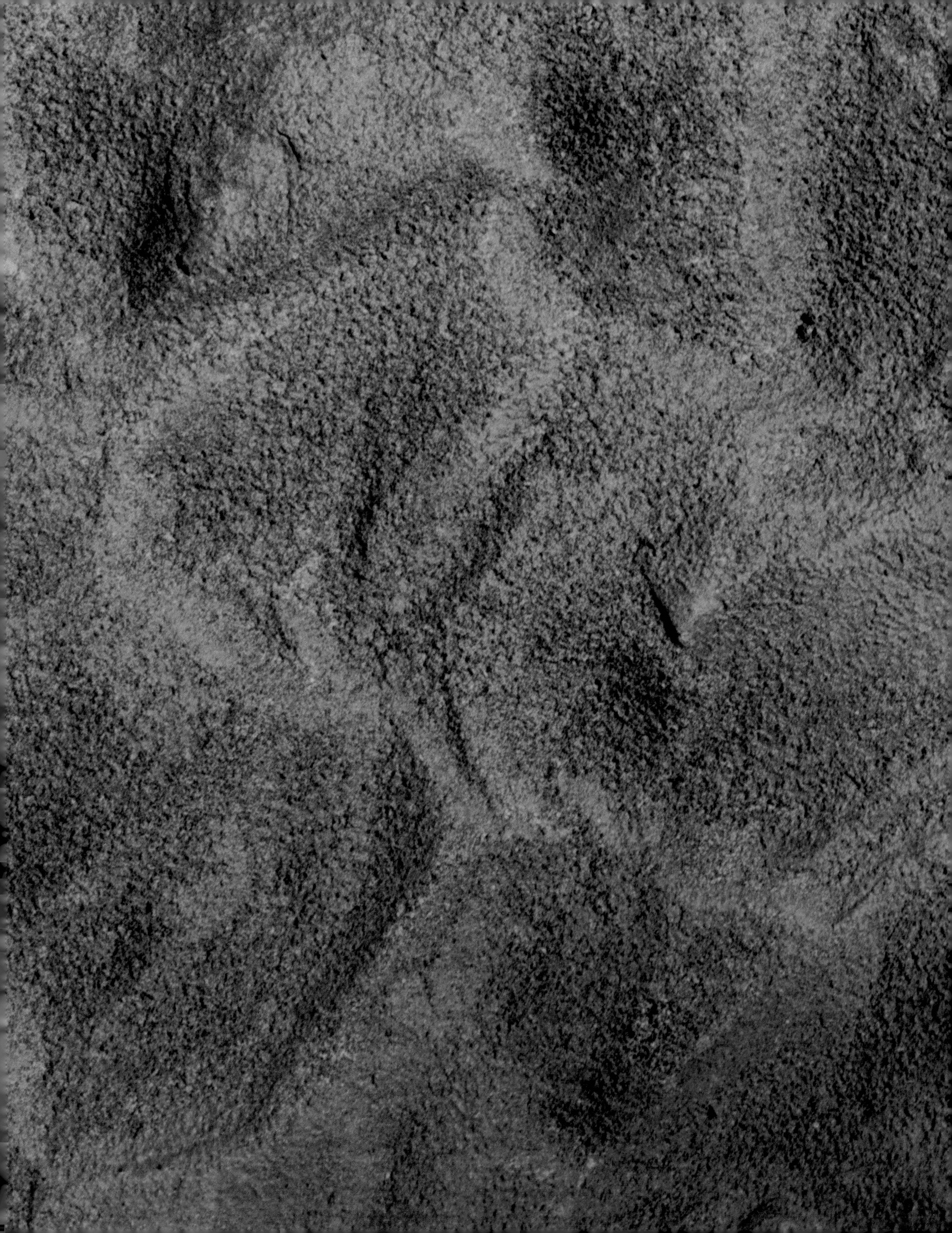

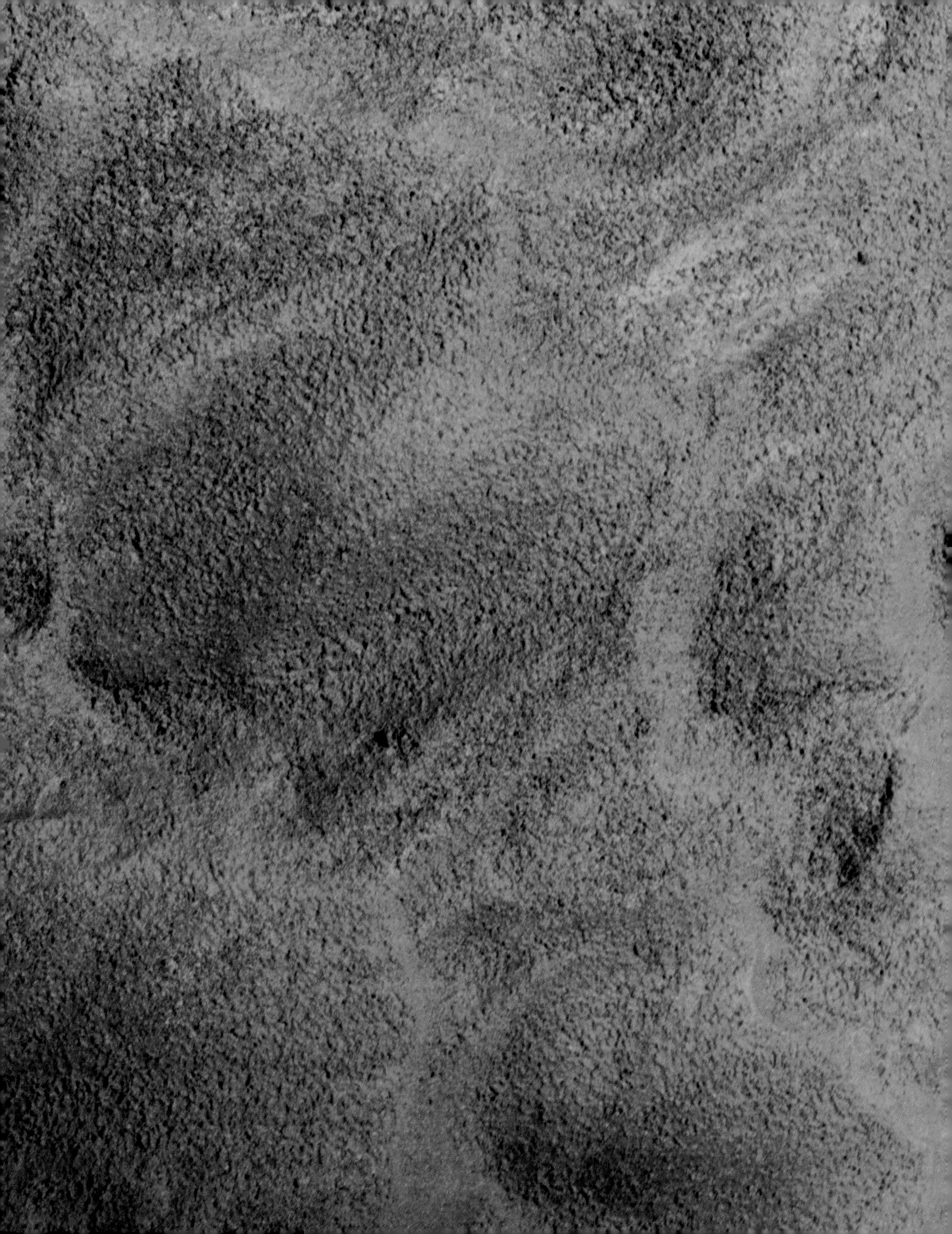

The images in frost are based on the series FROZEN EMBRYO SERIES 1991–2000,
STRANGLED BODY 1996–2000, and EROSION 1991–2001. They were reworked for
this book between 2000 and 2001. The typographic images refer to Hans Danuser's
word-text installations at Kunsthaus Zurich / Switzerland in 1996, at the Biennale
Lyon / France in 1997, and at Fotomuseum Winterthur / Switzerland in 2001.

"Nursery rhymes are attempts to structure children's world and play, providing a
model of and structure for the flow of life. Scientific models do the same, even if
they do not sound as poetic as 'eenie, meenie, miney, mo.'"

(Urs Stahel, *Topographies of Power*)

Hans Danuser frost

Design: Hans Danuser, Hanna Koller, Zurich
Scans, Printing, Production: Steidl, Göttingen

© 2001 for the images: Hans Danuser
© 2001 for this edition: Scalo Zurich - Berlin - New York

Head office: Weinbergstrasse 22a, CH-8001 Zurich / Switzerland
phone 41 1 261 0910, fax 41 1 261 9262
e-mail publishers@scalo.com, website www.scalo.com

Distributed in North America by D.A.P., New York City;
in Europe, Africa and Asia by Thames and Hudson, London;
in Germany, Austria and Switzerland by Scalo.

This book is published on the occasion of the exhibition *Hans Danuser—frost*
at Fotomuseum Winterthur, November 9, 2001, to January 6, 2002.

Main sponsor of the exhibition: Winterthur Insurance

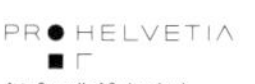 We would like to acknowledge the generous support of
Pro Helvetia, Arts Council of Switzerland.

We also express our thanks to culture promotion, Canton of Grison.

First Scalo Edition 2001
ISBN 3-908247-54-3
Printed in Germany